UNMOTHERED

A MEMOIR

KIM MURPHY

Kestrel House Press

Copyright © 2026 by Kim Murphy

All rights reserved.

No part of this book may be reproduced, stored in a retrieval system, or transmitted in any form or by any means—electronic, mechanical, photocopying, recording, or otherwise—without the prior written permission of the publisher, except for brief quotations used in reviews or scholarly works.

Published by Kestrel House Press

Millville, Delaware

kestrelhousepress.com

ISBN: 979-8-234-03001-6 (paperback)

ISBN: 979-8-218-92871-1 (ebook)

Printed in the United States of America

This memoir is a work of creative nonfiction. I have written true events from my life to the best of my recollection, changing some names to protect privacy. Events and time also may have been compressed for narrative clarity.

CONTENTS

For anyone who grew up too early.

PART ONE

Chapter 1

As my mother has declined, she's become harmless.

It doesn't erase forty years of hurt and resentment. But it's easier to be around her now because twelve or so years into her dementia diagnosis, she's bedbound and uncommunicative. I'm finally no longer afraid of her.

Every few months, I fly from Virginia to California to visit her and my stepfather, Dell. Mom can't speak and no longer recognizes me. I stand in her makeshift bedroom beside the hospital bed that's replaced the coffee table and couch in the den where they used to watch TV. I admire the smoothness of her skin or get lost in the endless to-do list rattling around in my head. Occasionally, she startles me by bolting upright and growling. Mostly she lays there with her eyes closed. After ten minutes, I get bored and wander back to the kitchen table and my laptop.

For years, I yearned for her, for her attention, for her time. Yet these days, despite how weak and frail she is——despite how different she is from the woman who raised me—I don't want to be with her. I wish I were inspired to stroke her hair or hold her hand. Or to crawl up in the bed. Shouldn't being with our mothers be the safest, easiest place to be? A place where we experience a deep sense of belonging matched only by our fear of losing them?

We didn't have that type of relationship. She wasn't that kind of mom. The fact that she's become quiet and docile doesn't change our past and all we've been through.

Last year, Dell told a social worker he thought Mom was still punishing me. That she was intentionally ignoring me during my visits. Giving me the silent treatment like she'd always done. "Punish" being the accepted euphemism for what we've never said aloud: abuse.

While Mom was manipulative and calculated before she lost her mind, even I didn't think she could override the ravages of dementia. Even I didn't believe she was capable of inflicting pain from her deathbed. I dismissed Dell's assessment, choosing instead to believe that whatever motivated her to be cruel, neglectful, and mean when she was in her right mind was gone. She'd become vacant and disengaged because her brain was dying. Her body would eventually follow.

• • •

It's now two years later, and my husband, Harry, and I are driving down I-95 to watch our younger son's college lacrosse game. Through the passenger window, the oak and hickory trees of Virginia slowly recede into the loblolly pines and red maples of North Carolina. My phone chirps from my purse. It's Dell.

"Hon, it looks like your mom is going to pass soon. I don't know if you want to fly out..." His voice trails off.

Mom's been in hospice care for eighteen months or so—first at home and now at a facility. Only she could defy the norms of hospice, which grants services only to those who're expected to die within six months. Because she's still alive—that is, alive and living, rather than alive and dying—the hospice administrators question whether she should continue receiving services. Somehow, though, each time they conduct a quarterly evaluation, Mom requalifies for another few months of services.

I've anticipated this phone call for months, if not years, yet I'm unprepared to give Dell an answer. Do I want to be with her in those final moments when I've spent much of my adult life trying to distance myself from her?

I assume someone who'd had a loving, caring, attentive mother would run to be with her. But what about people like me? What do we owe a parent at the end of their life when they failed to care for and love us as children?

Maybe the answer lies in what it means to be parented. To be loved by a mom or dad. And what it's like to *not* feel that love.

I promise Dell I'll call him later, then return to gazing at the trees whizzing by the window. In the silent pause, I imagine a sliding scale that stretches between abuse and neglect on one end to love and care on the other. With extreme abuse being at zero, there'd be no reason for an adult child to feel obligated. On the farthest end, at the one-hundred mark, there might be infinite reasons to show up. If anything, a person would be crushed *not* to be there. These are the people crawling up into the bed.

In the zero to fifty range, it gets messy. That's where Mom and I are.

Why would I decide to go? To fulfill some filial duty? To be free of guilt? To witness the death of hope and any notion that our relationship might change?

"What did he say?" my husband asks.

"It looks like she's going to die in the next couple of days. He asked if I want to be there. I'm not sure what to do. Do you think I should go?"

"What do *you* want to do?" He reaches over and grabs my hand, lacing his fingers in mine.

"I wish I did. Part of me wants it to be over already."

"What does the other part of you say?"

"That I should be there for Dell."

My chest clenches, squeezing all the air from my lungs as if my body is just now registering the situation. I begin sobbing for several minutes, tears and snot sliding down my face. I gulp air to steady myself but can't snag a big enough breath.

If I don't belong at her side, then where have I ever belonged?

Chapter 2

"Turn around so I can brush your hair."

Mommy pulls the brush from the top of my head down to my waist, through my long brown hair. My head snaps. I bring it forward, making a seesaw motion with every brush stroke.

I look down at my shoes. Black patent leather that squeaks when crossing the tile floor. Placing my right foot one half-step forward, I twist it back and forth to catch light so that it shimmers.

"My shoes are so shiny."

"Mm-hmm."

The brush snags a tangle of hair, jerking my head again.

"Hold still." She tugs, ripping through the knot. A loud crackle echoes in my ears. My scalp burns.

"*Ouch!*" I reach back instinctively to grab my hair.

"Stand still."

"Yes, ma'am."

"It's a special day. Don't you want to look pretty? Don't you want to make a good impression on the judge?"

I nod yes.

"Okay, then stop whining and let me finish."

I'm being adopted today. I don't know what that means, but I've been told Mommy's new husband, Tom, is going to be my new dad. Mommy says I'll still get to visit Larry, my real dad. I don't love Tom like I love Daddy.

Getting adopted means I'll have to change my last name. I don't want to do that because I've been practicing my letters, and I already know how to write "Kim Bradfield." Tom's last name is weird. It's hard to spell, and it's not a word you can sound out. We've learned how to do that in Mrs. Cardin's first-grade reading class. Mommy says some letters are silent. She says it's a Hungarian name. I need to practice printing and spelling it so that I can write it on my worksheets come Monday.

As I climb into the car to go to the courthouse, I smooth my skirt and tug my white tights to make the wrinkles disappear. I wonder what it'll be like to have two dads. Maybe it'll be double the fun, like in the Double Mint gum commercial with the twins.

• • •

I teeter on my tiptoes in the closet to reach my favorite jumper, giving it a swift yank off the hanger, which swings wildly. The jumper crumples into a pile on the floor; its big, bold fabric daisies form geometric patterns of bright yellow and deep black. I want to look pretty because my real daddy is coming to pick me up for the weekend. He has a new wife, my stepmother Carolyn. We're going to SeaWorld.

I run down the hall when the doorbell chimes. Daddy bends down to greet me with a hard hug as I throw my arms around his neck. He smells sweet and tangy, which makes my nose wiggle. I want to sniff it again, although I don't know why. He smells like a grown-up party I'm not allowed to go to. After a big twirl, he puts me down and takes my hand in his. Our arms swing together as we walk out the door. His thick, heavy class ring presses against my skin.

Carolyn sits in the front seat of the blue Volkswagen Beetle with the passenger door open. She pats her leg. "Hi, sweetheart. Come sit." Her smile makes my heart twinkle, the way ocean waves glitter beneath the sun. I scramble onto her lap, and her arms fold around me. It's so much better sitting up here with them rather than sitting alone in the backseat. I hope Mommy's not watching us drive away. She wouldn't be happy that I'm sitting up front.

Daddy drives as Carolyn rolls down the window. I extend my arm out into the warm wind, which forces my hand backward against the door frame. I fight to bring it forward.

"Can you catch colors out there?" Carolyn asks.

"Yes!"

I reach out, grab one from the air, and pull it inside the car.

"Here's red!" I say, unfolding my fist to show her. Her eyes brighten and she flashes a smile, her bright red lips framing perfectly white teeth.

"So pretty, sweetheart!"

"Here's purple!"

Again and again, I catch colors until a rainbow fills the car.

• • •

When the weekend ends, Daddy and Carolyn drive me home. Again, I sit up front on her lap. This time I'm not feeling sparkly. She runs her fingers through my hair, soft and gentle. Not rough the way Mommy brushes it. Once we arrive, Carolyn puts her arms around me and squeezes tightly.

"We'll see you again in two weeks, okay?" she says over my shoulder, then kisses my cheek.

When I hear the lilt in her voice, my throat fills with stones. I swallow hard, but they're stuck. My eyes sting as Daddy takes my hand and walks me to the front door.

He looks down and asks, "Why are you crying, honey?"

"I don't know," I squeak.

But I do know. I just can't say it. I worry that maybe, because Tom adopted me, Daddy will stop picking me up for our visits. If I don't get to see him, I also won't get to see Carolyn. I can't imagine not being able to sit on her lap or go on adventures with her anymore.

He rings the doorbell. I squeeze his hand and stare at my feet. Mommy opens the door.

"What's the matter? Why is she crying?" Her voice is sharp. She's wearing her mad face, the one where she pinches her eyebrows together and her eyes get small.

"I dunno. We had a great weekend," he says with a shrug.

She turns to me. "It's late. Go unpack your suitcase and put on your PJs." She sounds annoyed, her voice stiff and thin.

"Yes, ma'am." I squeeze past her down the hall and around the corner, stopping for a moment to listen to their conversation.

"I don't appreciate you bringing her home like this. She cries every time you drop her off."

"She was fine a few moments ago."

I don't want them to fight. I hate always having to say goodbye.

My cat, Rascal, follows me to the bedroom. With PJs on, I crawl into bed. Rascal jumps up and rubs the side of his cheeks on the bedspread. I stroke his fur. Purrs rattle his ribcage and tickle my hand. Scooping him closer, he curls up near my belly. I missed him.

• • •

Mommy climbs the ladder, reaching high above her head to loop strands of bulbs along the roofline. I shake loops of lights in my hand as if I'm playing a tambourine against my thigh.

"Don't do that! They're going to get tangled."

I continue handing up sections of lights. She reaches to the left, hooks a few more bulbs, climbs down, moves the ladder, climbs back up, hooks a few more. We repeat this pattern until all the lights are strung.

This is our first Christmas with Tom. Except he doesn't celebrate Christmas because he's Jewish. That means I'll get both Christmas and Hannukah presents this year.

I call Tom "Daddy" when I talk to him, but in my head, I call him Tom. He doesn't seem like a daddy. He doesn't have any other kids. He seems more like Mommy's husband, the man in our house.

Once we're done hanging lights, we head inside. Mommy lays tree branches cut from the bottom of our Christmas tree into the middle of our stone fireplace. Built into the front is a low bench made of rough rocks in shades of white and brown. I sit down, careful not to snag my pants. Mommy tucks twigs here and there, building a soft bottom layer for our holiday village.

We lift the lids on several shoeboxes and unfold the newspapers protecting our assortment of villagers. In one box, there are miniature pinecone people. Their cardboard feet prevent them from tipping over. Another box has angels dressed in red and gold foil dresses and white paper wings. Their heads look like wooden marbles. Some sing with mouths open, others close their eyes in prayer. Their gold halos wobble above their heads. In another box are crepe-paper Santas, with crinkly red suits and white-trimmed hats. In the fourth box is a herd of plastic reindeer.

I play with the angels, twisting their pipe-cleaner legs and arms, bending them this way and that and wrapping them around my fingers. With one wiggle, they bow like puppets.

When Mommy has finished laying down all of the tree branches, we place the angels, Santas, and reindeer one by one. We tie angels around twigs as if they're flying above the villagers and wedge reindeer between tufts of pine needles so that they don't topple. We work quietly side by side, then sit back to review our work. The scene is magical.

"It's so pretty, isn't it?" I ask.

"Mm-hmm"

She continues to fuss over the village without looking at me. I scoot closer, wishing she'd fuss over *me*. She is gentle with the reindeer, delicate with the angels. I want that tender touch on my hand or against my cheek.

I used to sit next to her on the couch when we watched TV, her hand resting on my knee. Now Tom sits beside her in my old spot. She used to read stories and tuck me in at night with a kiss. But I can read on my own, so we don't do that anymore.

As she rearranges angels, I can see in her eyes that she's busy in her head. Even when we're doing something together, like setting up the Christmas village, it's like we're doing it by ourselves. She's here and not here all at the same time.

• • •

When I'm eight years old, Daddy and Carolyn move from Northern to Southern California, which is a two-hour airplane ride from my home in Los Altos. I no longer see them every other weekend, which makes me sad if I think too much about it. But when I do visit, I stay longer, which I love. During school breaks and holidays, I fly by myself. No one else in my third-grade class gets to fly by themselves, have wings pinned to their shirts, or sit in the first row by the stewardesses.

When there on weekends, we go to Knott's Berry Farm, Disneyland, or Lion Country Safari. On weekdays, Carolyn and I play Yahtzee or Double Solitaire while Daddy's at work. She braids my hair as we watch *All My Children* and giggle during commercials. Just hearing her laugh makes me warm all over.

At the end of every workday, Daddy returns in dress slacks and a short-sleeved plaid button-down, drops his briefcase by the kitchen, and kisses Carolyn hello. They act like the married couples I see on TV. Like Carol and Mike Brady. Or Rob and Laura Petrie. But nothing like Mommy and Tom, who don't seem to like each other and argue most days.

Daddy picks me up with a hug. There's that sweet tangy smell again. I nuzzle my head into his neck, then lean back and hold his face in my hands.

"Hi, Daddy!"

When he smiles, I see the gold triangle on the tip of his front tooth. No one else I know has a gold tooth. His clear hazel eyes have brown flecks and thick blond lashes; they turn into half-moons when he laughs. Each time he smiles, my chest softens, like I've let out a deep sigh.

One morning, after Daddy goes to work, Carolyn teaches me to cook my favorite breakfast: French toast. She makes the best French toast.

She drags a stool over to the counter for me to stand on, then shows me each step. I break four eggs into a white bowl. With her hand over mine, we whisk eggs with a fork. After pouring milk into the bowl, we whisk some more. Then she takes four pieces of bread from the bag, two for each of us.

As the skillet heats up, I drop in two chunks of butter, watching them dance and sizzle.

"Use your fork to pick up the bread, and dip each side into the egg," she instructs.

"Like this?"

"Yep, that's perfect. Now lay it slowly in the pan."

I do as she says, careful not to splash egg juice everywhere. She knows I like the toast golden brown, so we wait and watch.

"See that steam coming up from the sides? That's a good sign they're done. We can take a peek."

She shows me how to use the fork to lift a corner to look underneath.

"Oh, they're perfect! Well done. Flip each one over. Let them cook a little longer. I'll get the plates."

We slather the French toast with butter, sprinkle powdered sugar on top, and carry our plates to the kitchen table. I pause before taking my first bite until after Carolyn takes hers. I watch as she cuts a few triangles and slides a forkful into her mouth. My eyes scan her face, eager to see a reaction.

"It's so yummy, sweetheart! Take a bite." She reaches across the table and grabs my hand. Her eyes grow wide, as she wrinkles her nose and smiles. "You did such a great job!"

My body melts and sizzles, like dancing butter.

• • •

I'm sandwiched between Rascal and the arm of our couch watching *The Courtship of Eddie's Father*. Eddie's supposed to be in fourth grade, one year older than me. He doesn't have a mom. Because she died, Eddie's always trying to get his dad to date. And get married.

Most of the families on TV don't look like mine. They have two loving parents and several children. Like *The Brady Bunch*. Or the mom is dead, and the dad is raising kids with the help of a maid, a butler, an uncle, or an aunt, like *Family Affair*, *The Andy Griffith Show*, and *My Three Sons*. Even Eddie's dad has Mrs. Livingston to cook dinner and wash clothes. Only *The Partridge Family* has a mom with no dad. But there are so many kids on that show that the older teens act like parents.

None of the people on TV are divorced and remarried. None of the kids shuttle between houses. They also never show parents yelling at each other; I mean, really yelling. The worst it gets is when Ricky scolds Lucy because she and Ethel are in trouble, but even then, the fight is funny.

In our house, there's nothing funny about the fighting. I hate it even though I'm used to it. Sort of. I figured out that some nights, I can be so focused on what Eddie, Buffy, or Jan and Marsha are doing that I don't notice the yelling.

Other times, there's no escape. Especially after I've gone to bed. That's when I stare at the ceiling, bite my nails, and tear at my hangnails until they bleed. My fingers, which are always raw and tender, sting when I eat salty foods.

On tonight's show, Eddie's gotten punched in the eye by a girl. Everyone decides she's a tomboy. They say she's "rough around the edges." Eddie's dad is so handsome and kind. He listens whenever Eddie talks. He wants to know how Eddie feels. He also wants to teach him how to defend himself.

When I hear voices rise from the kitchen behind me, I realize Mom and Tom are arguing. This time sounds different. Sharper. Louder. Lower. Their shrieks sound like the cat fights that break out beneath my bedroom window late at night.

I lean forward, straining to hear what Eddie's father is saying to Mrs. Livingston, but I can't hear a thing.

Tom stomps through the family room past me toward the front door. In seconds, Mommy storms by, a blur in my side vision.

"*Get out! Get out!*"

She lifts a frying pan over her head and crashes it downward, as if she's serving in a tennis match. He brings his arms up to cover his face, ducking sideways to avoid the smash.

"*Get out!*" She swings wildly at his head while he scrambles for the door handle.

"Mommy! *Stop!*"

She looks over in my direction.

"Go to your room!" she commands.

This is not her mad face. This is a face I've never seen before. Her lips press into a thin, hard line, like a straight ruler. Her eyes are wide and wild.

For a moment, I'm afraid she might come after me with the frying pan. I swipe at my cheeks to dry my tears, afraid that if she sees me cry, she'll become madder.

"*Now!*"

Her scream is hot and fiery. It thaws me from my frozen spot on the couch. I pick up Rascal, walk past the two of them squared off in the foyer, slip into my bedroom, and close the door. I stand stiff and stunned, unsure what to do. It's not bedtime yet. But I feel like crawling under the covers with Rascal until morning comes. I decide to change into my PJs, turn off the lights, and bury myself under the bedspread. Rascal settles in next to me. I stroke his head until I fall asleep.

The next day, there's no mention of the night before. No apologies. No explanations. Tom is still around. It's as if it didn't happen. Except in my head, where I replay the scene again and again.

A week later, Mommy and Tom sit me down in the dining room to say they're getting a divorce—even though they haven't been married all that long. I lower my head and pretend to be sad. Too bad I can't make myself cry. That's what they probably expect. Because who would be happy to hear their parents are getting a divorce?

Me! That's who. I've been hoping for this day. Tom's not my real dad. And whenever they're together, the air fills with anger, meanness, and noise. Their yelling makes me jumpy. I'm never as comfortable with them as I am elsewhere, like when I'm with Daddy and Carolyn at their house.

I pick at the frayed edges of the brown and gold place mat. They leave the table. I gaze at the ceiling and shake my fists.

"Yes!" I whisper. Now it can just be me and Mommy. And maybe she won't be mad all the time.

Chapter 3

I stand at the top of the driveway next to Rose, my next-door neighbor and babysitter. Since Mommy and Tom divorced a few months ago, there have been lots of babysitters. Mommy always has somewhere to go––night classes, bridge club, drinks with friends, dinners with men.

Tonight, it's Phil. I overheard Mommy tell her friend that he's married. I don't understand how that's possible. Doesn't being married mean you don't date other women?

I don't know much about him except he's a painter. He painted Mommy sitting on the floor, showing her backside. Naked. The painting hangs in her bedroom. Another shows her bent over, leaning on her knee, wearing a tennis dress. That's in our family room.

As Mommy walks past us to Phil's car, we're clouded in the salty caramel scent of Shalimar perfume. Her hips bump back and forth with each step while her long, jet-black hair sways side to side. If this were TV, you'd hear background music––*boom, bah-dah boom, bah-dah boom boom boom.* People say she looks like Cher.

I notice my neighbors, Ricky and Steven, who are in fifth grade and two years older than me, perched across the street on their Schwinn bikes. Several times a week they ride up to our house, kick-stop their bikes, and wait for a glimpse of her. As if she's a young, glamorous movie star.

In our neighborhood, she stands out because she's not like the other moms. She has a job but not as a teacher or a nurse. She's an aerospace engineer who works with rockets. Or maybe it's spaceships. She wants to be the first woman astronaut.

When she goes out at night, she looks so much softer than she usually does at home with me. Her brows aren't pinched. She smiles. She looks beautiful.

"Be a good girl," she calls back to me.

I nod.

After opening the car door, she slides into the passenger seat. The slit on her maxiskirt falls to one side, showing her tan legs. Bending forward to scoop up her skirt, the side of her breast pokes out from a gap in her halter top. Ricky and Steven grin at each other.

Will they––or anyone––ever look at me that way? Like in the cartoons when they get girl crazy and their eyes bulge out, their feet fly off the ground, and tweety birds and hearts dance around their head?

Phil starts the engine and drives away. The boys hop on their bikes and pedal off.

"Are you hungry?" Rose asks.

"Not really."

I am though, but not for what awaits. Another TV dinner. Swanson's Salisbury steak covered in brown gravy with mashed potatoes, a dried brown roll, and corn that tastes like gum wrappers.

This has been the routine since Tom left. We no longer sit as a family in the dining room. It's usually just me with the Salisbury steak on a TV tray, sitting next to a babysitter.

I wish Mommy would just stay home, be more like the other moms. If she won't do that, at least maybe take me with her wherever she goes.

I flip the channel to *The Brady Bunch* while Rose flips the pages of *Tiger Beat* magazine.

• • •

One night, Mommy can't find a babysitter. She tells me I need to come with her. I'm excited to see where she and her friends go and what they do. Yet when we walk into the gray building in downtown San Francisco, she says I'm not allowed to go inside.

"Stay here. Don't move. I won't be long," she says, disappearing behind the black door. She leaves me standing on the third-floor steps inside the building's stairwell. Despite floor to ceiling windows, it's as dark in here as it is outside. I smash my nose against the glass to look at the sidewalk below.

Men in hats and overcoats and women in heels and fur stream in and out of the building. None of their faces are clear. I imagine that couple is rich and lives in a fancy house in San Francisco, maybe near Fisherman's Grotto No. 9—my favorite restaurant. Those two are royalty, visiting from a faraway place where they have butlers, maids, and a Mary Poppins nanny to care for their five children.

But who are they really? Are they young like Mommy? Are they married or divorced? Do they have children? And if so, where are they? I never see kids in the places Mommy takes me.

Occasionally, the black door swings open, allowing me to peek inside.

I recognize the costumes the waitresses are wearing. They're Playboy Bunnies in black outfits, black stockings with diamond patterns, poufy hair, matching bunny ears, and fluffy cotton tails. Bright lips match painted fingernails. I've seen them in magazines that Tom hid under their bed. Here, they float through the crowd with drink trays perched on their shoulders. The umbrella drinks remind me of the Shirley Temples I have at restaurants with Daddy and Carolyn. Instead of being here in the stairwell, I wish I were with them snuggling on their couch.

Couples spill out the door. Men slap one another's backs and laugh as they stumble onto the stairs. All seem surprised to find me. I stare at my shoes or turn toward the window to avoid eye contact. Hopefully, no one will ask: *What are you doing? Where's your mom and dad? Shouldn't you be home in bed?*

I'm not here by choice, but it's clear I don't belong. My stomach tightens, as if I'm about to get in trouble.

As the night gets later, the voices get louder. Although they're shouting, they're also laughing. But they no longer appear fresh and fancy. Red lipstick is faded, curled hair falls limp. Men's ties hang sideways on their necks. They light cigarettes, reminding me of Tom.

Without my Snoopy watch, I don't know what time it is. Is it past bedtime? It must be. With that thought, I begin to worry. Where's Mommy? What happens if she doesn't come out? What if someone grabs and drags me down the stairs? My heart pounds in my throat.

After this experience, I no longer want to tag along. I'd much rather stay safe at home with a babysitter and eat Salisbury steak on a TV tray.

Chapter 4

I cuddle her gently, staring down at her button nose. Her lashes are long and thick, like Daddy's. She smells of warm cotton, baby powder, and honey. She's the best Christmas present I've ever received.

"You're such a good big sister," Carolyn tells me.

Me. Becoming a big sister, a month after my ninth birthday. Her name is Kerry.

Carolyn and I bathe and wrap her tight in yellow blankets. Comb her hair with a small, soft brush. We hang a new stocking so that Santa will know we are now a family of four.

In the mornings, Daddy goes to work and Carolyn and I make French toast. We also fill the hummingbird feeders. Carolyn taught me how to stand completely still with my arm outstretched and a dab of sugar water at the end of my pointer finger so that they'll take sips off it. It's hard not to move when they hover above me. My body bubbles and fizzes, like a shaken-up soda; I might pop from the excitement.

In the afternoons while Kerry naps, Carolyn and I watch *All My Children*. Carolyn is nothing like the stepmothers I see on TV or in the movies, all of whom are evil and mean. Carolyn acts the way real moms do. Or the way real moms are *supposed* to.

Being with her is like sinking into an oversize beanbag. It makes me never want to leave. Because it's soft and safe. *She* is soft and safe. She loves me and wants to spend time with me. My wish that Daddy and Mommy were still married is no more. Instead, I wish Carolyn was my real mom and that this was my everyday home.

Today, we decide to watch *Stella Dallas,* an old movie made before Carolyn was born. In the story, Stella and Stephen get married after dating only a short time. They have a baby, Laurel. Stephen works far away, so Laurel sees her Dad only sometimes. They go on vacations and adventures together. It reminds me of all the adventures Daddy and I have gone on when I've visited.

As the story continues, Stephen—even though he's still married to Stella—meets and falls in love with another woman, Helen. Laurel meets Helen and they get along great, far better than Laurel does with her mom, Stella. Laurel is confused by her feelings for Helen, and for her mom. Just like I'm confused by my feelings for Carolyn and Mom.

For the first time, I'm seeing my life echoed in a movie. In one scene, while Laurel and Stella take a train ride, Laurel is embarrassed when she overhears other passengers talking badly about her mom. I've felt that too. I know moms in the neighborhood talk about Mommy, "the young divorcée." It embarrasses me but also makes me want to protect her. I don't want her feelings hurt. Yet, I also don't want to be the daughter of someone other people talk about or don't like.

After Stephen and Stella divorce, Stella pretends to reject Laurel. She does that hoping that Laurel can go live with Stephen and be raised by the more glamorous Helen. Laurel grows up and gets engaged. She invites Stella to the wedding, but when Stella fails to respond, Helen tells her there must be a mistake. Her mother wouldn't reject her like that. Helen is so kind, comforting, and loving. She never talks badly about Stella.

In the final scene, Laurel marries Richard in the mansion, believing her mother isn't there. But Stella is there, outside in the pouring rain. Dripping wet, with her hair pasted to her face.

She's watching her daughter's wedding from a window.

At that moment, all of the air leaves my body. My head buzzes with confusion and questions. I'm overcome with tears that fall hard and heavy, so hard that I can't breathe.

If I love Carolyn more than Mommy, or wish that she was my real mom, am I destroying my relationship with Mommy? Would she care enough to watch my wedding from a window? Or would she turn her back on me? And what would happen if I'm ever confused about or misunderstand Mommy's actions, like Laurel misunderstood Stella? As sad as the movie is, it also scares me.

Carolyn is crying too.

We sit side by side, weeping and blowing our noses. She reaches over to take my hand. I look up at her. We cry harder. Snot. Salt. Sobs.

But then, we start to giggle. Softly at first. Until laughter erupts and overtakes the tears.

"I can't believe we're crying so much," she says with a laugh.

"Me either. That was so sad!" As soon as I speak, more tears come. I wipe my eyes with a crumpled, soggy tissue.

That night, I think more about Stella, Laurel, and Helen. I know my family is unusual. Two dads. Two moms. Marriages. Divorces. Visitations. Multiple homes. There are no families like ours on TV or in the movies, no characters who deal with the same situations and feelings I have. The conflicts. Embarrassment. Confusion. Fear. Sadness. The wishing for a different life, a different kind of family. No one speaks the things I can't tell anyone else about.

I feel an odd comfort in watching Laurel struggle. Despite not knowing anyone with divorced parents, if there's a story out there like mine, then someone else must have had these same types of thoughts and experiences. Still, the movie doesn't offer answers on how to handle such confusion and divided loyalties. It only makes me worry that someday I might marry without Mommy, while she stands in the rain, watching from a window.

Chapter 5

Jim's wearing jeans and a red flannel shirt. He twirls the blade of grass he's been chewing on, smiling at me with ice blue eyes. I love the thin crinkly lines that form on the tops of his cheeks. He's even more handsome than Mr. Eddie's Father. When he looks at me, I hear those tweety birds dancing around my head. It's good that I like Jim so much because he's been Mommy's boyfriend through all of my fourth-grade year.

We spend weekends at his farmhouse in the country town of Fall River beneath the shadow of Mount Shasta. He teaches me to launch clay pigeons for target practice in the back fields near the old outhouse. Early Saturday mornings in summer, the three of us gear up in waders, plop into inner tubes, and float down the river so that Mommy and Jim can fly-fish. I lay back in my tube, staring at the sky, dangling my hand in the icy water, swishing it back and forth to make the tube spin. My scalp and ponytail burn beneath the sun. Fish swim under and around my tube. The water is so clear, I can count the rocks at the bottom of the river ten feet below.

In winter, we go to Jim's cabin in Tahoe to ski. I master standing at the bottom of lift lines yelling "Single!" to find other skiers to pair up with on the chairlift to the mountain top. At day's end, we meet by the ski lodge. I shift my weight to the right and then to the left to pop out of my skis, unbuckle the tops of my bright-orange ski boots, and clomp closely behind Mommy and Jim with skis hoisted on my shoulder as we walk back to the car.

This week, we're in Idaho to ski at Sun Valley. Since we arrived, Mommy and Jim have been skiing during the day and going out to listen to music at night. I ski during the day, but at night, I'm either in my room watching TV or in the lobby by the fireplace curled up in the huge maroon leather chairs reading or drawing.

I like being away from home because when we're at home, I have to follow a long list of rules:

Respond with "yes, ma'am" or "no, ma'am."

No sass or backtalk.

Make your bed.

Do your chores.

Clear your plate.

No dessert until you've finished your dinner.

Wash your dishes.

Put your toys away.

Feed Rascal and Whiskers the guinea pig.

Do your homework.

Study your French lessons.

Practice your piano.

No playing in the living room.

No feet on the couch.

Keep your napkin in your lap.

No chewing with your mouth open.

Hold your knife and fork properly.

Act like a young lady.

Answer the phone with the proper greeting.

And absolutely *no lying!*

But when we're away, most of the rules vanish. There are no chores or homework to worry about. There's no babysitter watching over me. And Mommy is off with Jim, so I can do what I want.

Tonight, I'm bored. I finished my book, don't feel like drawing, and there's nothing good to watch on TV. I'm also hungry. So, I grab my red rubber coin purse, which holds two dollars in quarters, and go to the lobby for a snack.

I poke my head inside the restaurant and peer around the corner where the vending machine sits. A paper sign taped to the front reads: OUT OF OR-DER. Disappointed, I wander inside the restaurant, looking left, then right. Should I ask the waiter for some chips or french fries? Should I walk to the corner store to see if it's open?

While standing there tapping my coin purse against my leg, two men seated at the bar notice me.

"Need help?" one of them asks.

"The vending machine is broken. I was going to buy some chips or candy."

They ask me several other questions, which I answer politely. I know how to talk to grown-ups and how to act around them. Because I don't live with brothers or sisters, I'm around adults more than kids. And I'm comfortable talking to and being around men because Mommy is never without one.

"Here," one of them says, as he scoots a stool closer. "Come sit. We'll buy you a burger and some chips. Want a soda?"

"Really? Thanks!"

I climb up, excited that they're being so nice. It feels grown-up to sit at the bar.

They ask me more questions. I ask them some too.

They're from San Francisco, which isn't far from where I live. They're both married and have kids. One has a nine-year-old just like me.

In the bathroom mirror at home, I've been practicing some of the facial expressions I see women on TV make when they're talking to men. Like when Marlo Thomas in *That Girl* crinkles her nose at Don when something's funny. Or she tilts her head to the side, eyes big and watery like a cartoon deer, with a half-smile at the corner of her mouth.

From my spot on the stool, I crinkle my nose and tilt my head. And when the burger comes, I place my napkin in my lap (Rule No. 15) and am careful not to talk with my mouth full (Rule No. 16).

The men invite me to go see the movie *Billy Jack* the next day at the resort's theater. I must be doing well with my manners. Otherwise, why would they ask?

At home, I watch Mommy's face to see if I'm behaving correctly. Maybe I'm talking too much. Or being too silly. When she doesn't like what I'm doing, her forehead wrinkles, her eyes go black, and her mouth drops. The bone on the side of her jaw wiggles back and forth. Sometimes I can't tell what I'm doing wrong. But I recognize the warning face that comes before the mad face.

When I see it, I stop what I'm doing and am extra quiet, as if I'm not in the room. I make myself disappear without going anywhere. If I can do that, sometimes she won't get too mad. And she'll stop saying "young lady," which I hate hearing because it's the warning that comes before the yelling, the spanking, and the order to "Go to your room."

Since she's not here, it's hard to know if I'm behaving as I should. It's not easy to look at other people's faces and know what they're thinking. Still, I'm always trying to figure it out.

The guys are smiling. Laughing. Paying attention. Not ignoring me. So I don't think I'm being bad. If I am, they don't seem to mind.

The next morning, I tell Mommy I don't feel like skiing. She doesn't ask why or argue that I have to go with them. Which is good. She just zips up her snow pants and heads to the slopes. After she leaves, I'm excited to do something fun.

My heart thumps faster knowing I'm also doing something I probably shouldn't. I just hope Mommy doesn't find out or I'll be in real trouble. For what exactly, I'm not sure. But she'll find a way to be mad about it.

A few hours after Mommy leaves, I meet the guys in the lobby after lunch to walk the short path to the theater. Every place in Sun Valley is like a scene from a Christmas movie. The theater looks like it's from an old-timey postcard photo. There are huge stone walls, a high triangle roof, and fresh snow twinkling under the bright sun. Next to the red double doors is a movie poster taller than me showing Tom Laughlin as Billy Jack in a black hat and black T-shirt. He looks serious and scary.

The guys buy me a soda and popcorn. We settle into our seats, with me in the middle. No one else is in the theater. Almost as soon as the movie begins, I know Mommy wouldn't want me watching the way Billy Jack uses his bare feet to karate-chop the bad guys. But I'm not worried about having to tell her how I spent the day because she doesn't ask what I do when she's not around. She's not that interested.

What's that saying? "Out of sight, out of mind." That's how it might be for Mommy. I think she wants me out of sight, out of mind at all times, even when I'm standing right in front of her.

Chapter 6

In the middle of fifth grade, Mom decides to transfer me from Pinewood, the small private school I've attended since kindergarten, to the local public school around the corner. There's no discussion or explanation about her decision; there never is. She does what she wants without regard to others—especially me.

I like Pinewood. Most days after school, I go to the art room with Mrs. Jenson. We glue strips of paper and fabric onto empty jars using Mod Podge. We mix tempera paint into old coffee cans, then paint canvases with large brushes. We string beads into bracelets. Usually, it's just the two of us because no other kids have moms who work.

On Tuesdays, rather than going to the art room, I walk through the orchard behind the school to my music teacher's house for singing lessons. Ms. Shay hugs me hello and goodbye, smelling of cinnamon and butter, as if she's been baking cookies. When was the last time Mom hugged me? It's not each time she sees or leaves me. I love hugs, especially ones that make my insides ooze like warm honey melting into the nooks and crannies of an English muffin.

One random February day, I'm a new student at Oak Elementary and everything changes. Now, I walk to school rather than have Mom drive me. When I walk home, I let myself into the house using a key tied to my lunchbox. There's now a new rule: Call Mom as soon as I get home.

Sometimes, if she's been busy at work, she'll call me. I must answer, "Vajta residence, Kim speaking." She replies by saying, "This is the Wicked Witch of the West calling."

The Wizard of Oz is my all-time favorite movie. Why does she choose the Wicked Witch rather than the beautiful, dreamy Glinda the Good Witch? I don't get it, but I respond by laughing so that she doesn't fall into a mood.

It takes a while to adjust to the new routine. No more art or singing. No more Tuesday hugs. Only a French tutor who comes Thursdays for an hour. And she's not a hugger.

During the first few weeks, I go straight to my bedroom, missing everything about Pinewood and how I used to spend my afternoons. But I have the best bedroom. I don't mind being sent there when I'm punished. It's bright and cheery and filled with piles of art supplies, books, dolls, and stuffed animals.

I stretch on my tiptoes to reach the long white shelves where my doll collection sits. Mom buys them at the gas station for ninety-nine cents when she fills up the car with gas—as long as I've been a good girl. I have a full set of twelve that sits next to my collection of high-stepping plastic horses.

Each wears clothing to reflect their country. I grab the yellow-haired doll from Ireland. She's in a gold ballgown stitched with shamrocks and green sparkles. I tilt her back and forth, watching her eyes open and close. The doll from Spain wears a deep red ballgown trimmed with black lace and a matching veil. Today, Ireland and Spain play with Lady Eskimo, who's in tan boots and a brown, full-length furry hooded coat.

Putting the dolls aside, I grab my oldest friend: an unnamed, pink floppy-eared one-eyed bunny, worn thin by years of cuddling. I lean back to rest against Bear, who is four feet tall and too big to fit on the shelves. Bear lives on my bed. Rascal curls up inside Bear's outstretched legs, and I prop myself against him to read. It's only when Mom returns home that I realize how long I've been in my room alone.

• • •

Within a few weeks at the new school, I realize I've been dropped into an entirely different world. At Pinewood, girls thought boys had cooties. They chased us; we ran. At Oak Elementary, they talk of French kissing and first and second base. Girls want the boys' attention rather than to run from them. I have a lot to learn, and I need to do it quickly because I refuse to be so clueless that I get teased or made fun of.

I want to fit in. Yet there are already a million reasons that I stand out: my divorced parents, my working mom, my French lessons, my weird last name, my lack of siblings. And I hate all the questions: *Why did your parents divorce? Why were you adopted? Why is the "J" silent in your name? Why does your mom work? Why? Why? Why?*

One day, while lining up for class, a boy I haven't spoken to slides me a note. It reads: WILL YOU GO STEADY WITH ME? I don't even know this kid, but I want him—along with anyone and everyone—to like me. Too afraid to say no, I nod yes. His smile widens, as I wonder: *What does going steady mean, exactly?*

That afternoon, girls in my class ask, "You like Orin?" Their squished noses, crinkled cheeks, and raised voices make it clear that Orin is unpopular. I interpret their reaction as my clue to change course. Now. Going steady with Orin is not a path to being liked or making friends. The next morning, I return a note telling him I don't want to go steady anymore. He reads the note, crumples the paper, and tosses it in the trash, never looking back in my direction. I feel bad but not that bad.

Around the same time, Mom decides I no longer need babysitters. She decides I'm capable of being on my own—not only after school, but also at night. I am ten. She doesn't explain why, assuming I'll accept any change thrown my way. A new boyfriend for mom. A new school for me. There are never any discussions.

But there's also another new rule: *No friends in the house when she's not home.*

For the most part, I do as I'm told. There's no reason to break rules or skip chores and suffer consequences like losing privileges. Or the worst consequence: having her stop speaking to me—not just for a little while, but for hours or even a whole day.

I mistakenly thought that with Tom out of the picture, she would be better. Quieter. Calmer. Because I don't remember much about life before

Tom, I assumed the constant tension in our house was caused by their rela-tionship. If he was out of the house, she would be more like the mom who hosted my fifth birthday party, strung the pinata on the back patio, and laughed when I swung and missed. Maybe she'd be more like the mom who kissed me on the cheek and used to tuck me in at night. Or the one who took me to the fabric store to pick brightly colored patterns and sewed my grade-school jumpers. Where did *that* mom go?

Now she scowls so often that there are two deep lines carved into the skin between her brows—like exclamation marks between her eyes. It's not clear why she's mad all the time. Is it me? Or someone and something else? Since there isn't anyone else, it must be me.

I don't like it when she's mad. Hearing one note of exasperation in her voice, I pop to attention, scrambling to see what I can do to change her mood. I clear plates from the table without being asked, rinse dishes and place them into the dishwasher. I brag about a check plus on an assignment or being chosen for the spelling bee. None of it works.

I learn to read her moods just by the *slap, slap, slap* of her slippers on the floor in the morning. Hard heel strikes and crisp sounds mean stay out of her way. If she's agitated, I disappear into my room. Soft, muffled claps mean she's in a good mood. If she's chatty, I join in. I change colors in her presence, like a chameleon avoiding danger.

When she announces I no longer need babysitters, I'm excited. I don't mind being home alone, at least not during the day. It's better than being on edge when she's around. Having babysitters is okay, but they don't pay much attention to me either; they're too busy talking to boyfriends on the phone or reading *Teen* or *Tiger Beat* magazines. Because I already know how to cook TV dinners, I don't need help for that either. How hard can it be to take care of myself?

Initially, I follow her rules. I also spend a lot of time alone. It's not just after school. Many nights, she's out with friends or with Jim or at bridge club. Maybe I don't need to be such a strict rule follower. No one else is around. Who's going to know?

At first, I lie about washing my hair, about eating bowls of ice cream with my feet on the couch, about watching TV rather than doing homework.

Once, she tips my head down and digs into my scalp to see if I'm telling the truth about washing my hair, but mostly, I don't get caught and nothing bad happens.

• • •

I become friends with three kids on my block. We walk to school together, cutting through yards and picking Bing cherries off the trees. With so much alone time, I'm eager to be with other kids. I invite them over to my house when Mom's not home.

One Saturday, as Mom cleans the fireplace, she notices a sticky, golden residue on the raised stone hearth. She calls down the hall.

"Kim! Come here *immediately*." I put down the toy I'm playing with and run to the family room. Judging by the screech in her voice, she's furious.

"What is this?" She points to the telltale signs of the fire my friends and I made while we were playing with matches.

"I don't know."

"You most certainly do, young lady. What is this?" Jaw clenched, her mouth barely opens as she growls.

I remember this look. The one I saw the night she went after Tom with the frying pan, her face red and contorted. I squeak out a confession, heart racing. Tiny beads of sweat form in the center of my palms. I explain all my infractions: the friends over, the matches, the piling of paper on the hearth, the fire, the stamping it out.

"You could have burned down this whole house!" she screams.

In one sweeping motion, she grabs my arm, whips me around, and strips my pants and underwear to my ankles. Surprised by her strength, I feel embarrassed and far too old for a bare-bottomed spanking. Plus, it's been a long time since I've been spanked at all.

"I'm sorry, I'm sorry, I'm sorry."

I twist and turn, trying to wiggle a hand to cover myself so that the spanking won't hurt as much. Catching my wrists with one hand, she yanks both arms overhead.

"Hold still!" she commands. This is no ordinary spanking. It's not three whacks. She hits repeatedly. Again and again. The burn of each next slap worsening. When she's done, she's breathless and glaring. My whole body shakes beneath her stare. And everything stings, from my eyes to the backs of my legs. I'm afraid to move, in case she's not done yet.

Looking up at her, I don't recognize this mom. Not her face. Not her eyes. Not even her anger. It's true that I did something wrong; I broke the rules. But she's the one who's always gone. I wouldn't have played with matches, had friends over, or built the fire if she'd been here.

Maybe it's harder to take care of myself than I thought. Maybe I'm supposed to have someone around to make sure I don't do things I'm not supposed to. Why do I have to be both the child and my own parent?

"Now go to your room!"

I limp off, trembling but relieved the spanking is over. I fall on the bed, wrap my arms around Bear's leg, and sob into the pillow. I know making fires is wrong; I just want to do what my friends want to do. I want them to like me so that I don't have to spend so much time alone. I also don't want to be the one in charge, having to say, "No we can't do that. We'll get in trouble." Because kids don't like other kids who say those things. No one likes a kid who pretends to be a parent and is a no-fun rule follower. That won't ever be me.

Several hours pass until she calls me to dinner.

Dinner is served on plates at the kitchen table. Lima beans? Did she serve my most hated food on purpose? Anytime we have lima beans for dinner, there's a standoff. I refuse to eat them, and she won't allow me to leave the table until every bean is gone. Many nights, I push lima beans around the plate until bedtime. Some nights, I spit them into a napkin.

I've hated lima beans for so long. In third grade, I wrote a long note in cursive: "*I will never, ever, ever, ever, ever, ever, ever, ever, ever, ever, ever, ever like lima beans.*" Writing it demonstrated my seriousness about the issue. She vowed to save the note, convinced that I would someday change my mind. We were equally committed to being right.

Tonight, lima beans are a punishment. She doesn't say another word about the fire. In fact, she doesn't say another word the rest of the night. We sit in silence. When she finishes dinner, she gets up and clears her plate, while I push lima beans around until it's time for bed.

Chapter 7

The Oak Elementary girls can be mean. I'm willing to be mean too, as long as I can be friends with the three most popular girls in class: Lisa, Laurie, and Donna.

The four of us don't all hang out together. Instead, we rotate in an unspoken game of two against two. Lisa and I will be close friends for one week, while Laurie and Donna are connected. Overnight, the pairs switch. The friend we talked about behind their back on a Tuesday might be our best friend by Thursday. I never understand how, why, or when the switches occur. When they happen unannounced, I simply fall in line, hoping to remain in the circle.

To mark our elementary-school graduation, the entire sixth-grade class heads to a weeklong outdoor educational camp in the mountains. The plan is for Laurie and me to ride together and share the same bunkhouse.

Days before we're scheduled to leave, I catch bronchitis. On Saturday, the day Laurie's parents are to drive us, I'm sick in bed and unable to go. I stare at the ceiling, sad to miss the big adventure. On the window above my bed, which spans most of my bedroom wall, I hear a soft *tap, tap, tap*. I roll over to see Laurie smiling and waving, motioning for me to crank open the window.

"I'm so sad you can't come to camp!"

"Me too," I say, the words scratching my throat, forcing me to cough into my pillow. "Mom said if I get better, I might be able to go midweek."

"I hope so!" she beams. "Okay, gotta go."

"Okay, bye!" I flop back down on my bed, sweaty and feeling sorry for myself.

By Tuesday, I'm much better, and Mom agrees that I can go. Parents of another kid from class who was also sick will drive us.

Because I arrive late, I'm assigned another bunkhouse with three girls from different schools. They're playing cards on the top bunk. When I'm introduced by the counselor, they barely look up.

I set down my duffel bag and head out to find my classmates, especially Laurie. Everyone's in a clearing, sitting on logs and listening to the counselors announce the day's activities. We will be going down to the creek to look for salamanders, then hike to learn which plants are edible and which are poisonous.

Laurie's on the far side of the circle with Lisa and Donna. I wave, but none of them wave back. I crouch on a moss-covered log to listen. Maybe she didn't see me.

When the counselor finishes, I run to my friends.

"Hi!" I chirp, eager for hugs and squeals.

"Oh, hi," Laurie says, turning back around to Donna and Lisa.

In the time between Laurie's taps on my window and arriving at camp, I've been ousted. None of them speak to me for the rest of camp. I'm crushed though not surprised. It's clear now that if a friend will be mean or talk behind someone's back, there's no reason that so-called friend won't do the same to me.

My bunkmates are no better. They want nothing to do with me. By day two, they tease me about the way I flick my head to the side whenever my bangs fall into my face, which is basically all the time since I'm growing out my bangs. What began as an annoying habit is now a nervous tic that I can't shake.

Three days ago, all I wanted was to be at camp. Now that I'm here and not fitting in with anyone, all I want is to go home, back to the quiet calm of my own bedroom. What's the alternative to being stranded somewhere without friends?

I decide to learn what to do if I'm ever stranded without water, which is that afternoon's lesson. The steps are: Dig a hole, pee in it, set a cup in the middle, cover the hole with Saran wrap, and place a small rock on top. Liquid from the urine will evaporate, condense and drip into the cup. That's one way to survive.

When I return home, Mom also notices I'm flipping my bangs constantly as well as blinking my eyes. She takes me to Dr. Henderson to find out what's wrong.

"Stress!" he declares and sends us on our way.

No one asks why I'm stressed. No one wonders how a young girl could be so stressed. Not Mom. Not the doctor. No one considers how to get me unstressed.

• • •

Being rejected by Laurie, Lisa, and Donna isn't enough for me to stop wanting to be their friend. By the time we get home, they too have forgotten that they didn't want to be mine; we resume our many rounds of pairings through the summer until we start seventh grade at Blach Intermediate, the local junior high. Then everything changes permanently when we drift apart, find new friends, and go our separate ways.

One of my new friends in particular, Renee, becomes one of the first girls I really care about and who cares about me. I'm not drawn to her to fit in or be popular, which is the main reason I wanted to be liked by Laurie, Donna, and Lisa. Renee makes me laugh, and we can talk for hours.

We also write long notes and pass them back and forth between classes. We share secrets, detail our crushes, and give each other nicknames. She's Brown Eyes. I'm Brandy, inspired by the Looking Glass song.

On Career Day, we skip school. Because it's not a regular school day, attendance seems optional. At least by our calculations. We choose instead to walk around town and go to the corner store. Smoking our first cigarettes, we learn that if we don't inhale too deeply, we can avoid jagged coughing fits. We trek several miles to the construction site where her parents are building a new home, tromping around the lot until we lose interest and walk back into town. It's so much more fun than listening to presentations about accounting, lawyering, and doctoring.

•••

Just as I'm settling in and enjoying life at Blach, Mom announces we're moving cross-country to Virginia. She's taking a big important job at the Central Intelligence Agency. We'll move in January, after Christmas break, smack dab in the middle of seventh grade.

Once again, Mom doesn't discuss or explain her decision. She doesn't care how I might feel.

"Imagine, being in Washington, DC, during the Bicentennial!" she says, an odd soft and wistful tone in her voice.

There's nothing about that idea that intrigues me. I barely understand why the Bicentennial would even be a big deal. I can't imagine why she's so excited, and I don't ask.

Having never moved before or visited the East Coast, I'm also not sure what to expect. But, as usual, it doesn't matter what I think; I need to brace myself for the changes ahead.

•••

Shortly before we move, Carolyn calls Mom. It's not unusual for them to talk because they coordinate my visits. I assume they're talking about the upcoming Christmas holiday break.

My last visit was in August before school started. Carolyn and I, along with two-year-old Kerry, went to the beach nearly every day. During lunch at the yacht club, she told me how much she loved me and that we would always be family. No one has ever said anything like that to me before.

Sure, Mom tells me she loves me, but I don't believe her. I can count on Mom's love only if I behave and obey, if I'm a good girl. Her version of love disappears with the slightest infraction. I've begun to wonder, is that really love? If it involves making a deal, how can it be real? Shouldn't love be something you can depend on no matter what?

Plus, I'm not even sure Mom likes me. When I like someone, I'm curious about their thoughts, their interests, their likes and dislikes. I want to get to know them. Spend time with them. None of which Mom does. She folds me into her life when she has no other choice but to have me around.

Carolyn's words—we'll always be family—felt real. When I'm with Carolyn, there's no doubt she loves me, that she cares, that she likes me.

There are stark differences between Mom and Carolyn and how they each treat me.

After that lunch conversation, it was as if I were floating in the knowledge that no matter what, I would always have a safe and loving home with Dad, Carolyn, and Kerry. This makes up for so much of what is missing at home with Mom. Now that we're moving, I just need to realize that it'll take longer to fly from Virginia to California to see them. Other than that, not much else should change.

I sit on the black swivel stool in our kitchen, twisting back and forth, listening to Mom's side of the conversation with Carolyn. It's hard to tell what they're talking about. When Mom hangs up, she turns to me and says flatly, "Carolyn and Larry are getting a divorce."

"What? What do you mean?" Dinner comes back up in my throat. I swallow hard to keep myself from throwing up. My ears ring. The room tilts to the left. I grab the sides of the stool, worried I might fall.

How can this be? She just told me how much she loved me. That we would always be family. They were so happy a few months ago.

I'm confused and wonder if I misunderstood our conversation. How did I get that so wrong?

I love you so much, sweetheart. We will always be family. I love you so much, sweetheart. We will always be family.

I begin to wonder if her words were code for something else. What was she trying to say? What did she really mean?

For weeks, I replay our lunch conversation, in an attempt to make sense of it. Maybe when she said, "We will always be family," she meant she and I. The two of us, plus Kerry, will always be family. Maybe she didn't mean the four of us, as in Carolyn, Kerry, me and Dad.

She and Mom talk a few more times, and I begin to learn that Dad drinks too much. They say he's an alcoholic. It's not the first time I've heard this. It's just the first time I've actually thought about it. The stories Mom shares after speaking with Carolyn don't sound like Dad. Hidden bottles behind the toilet tank. Detox tremors. Failed rehabs. There are so many new words and concepts, I struggle to keep up.

The big question is: Now what? Do people stay close to a stepparent who is divorced from their real parent? I don't know anyone who has stepparents, so there's no one to ask.

Mom reassures me that I'll be able to visit them both. I'll spend time with Carolyn and Kerry at their home, and with Dad at his new apartment.

• • •

With the move to Virginia now just a week away, every day is an unfolding of endless hard goodbyes.

Mom won't allow me to bring all of my stuffed animals, dolls, or horses. She says there are too many to transport. I pull them down one by one from my bedroom shelves, deciding which to give away and which to take with me. As the bags and boxes pile up, I throw myself onto my bed and look at the empty walls of my room. There's no artwork on the bare bulletin board. No clothes in the closet. No dolls or horses on the shelves. The only telltale sign that this was my room are the three roller-blind shades on the windows. I slowly pull down each one to reveal the individual four-foot-high floral decal letters that spell my name: K-I-M. The shades that once towered over my kindergarten self now appear babyish. Those letters are for a little kid, not for someone who skips school and smokes cigarettes. Still, this room has been a haven—the safest, quietest place I know.

Thankfully, Mom allows me to take Rascal, but I have to say goodbye to Whiskers, my eight-year-old guinea pig. I carry him to the pet store, begging the pet store owner to take him.

"Guinea pigs only live for five years or so," he explains.

"But I don't have anywhere else for him to go," I plead. Finally, he agrees, and I make the sad walk home by myself, an empty cage swinging side to side, banging my leg.

I say goodbye to Jim, hugging him hard around the neck and wiping tears away with my T-shirt sleeve. I know it's likely I'll never see him again. How could they date if they live on opposite sides of the country? So, I assume leaving California means Mom's also leaving Jim. I'm expected to just get over it, as if he's meant nothing to me these past four years.

I don't want to think about it. It's not helpful and changes nothing. In situations like this, or perhaps in every situation, Mom's work and her wants are more important than anything else. Way more important than anything I might want or need. Adjusting to her decisions means falling in line. Pouting or crying will only anger her. And I know well the consequences of that.

This time though, the changes, the expectations are too much for me. How can I endure all of these final goodbyes all at once?

On the last day I attend school, I sit on the radiator in the back of science class as Renee and I exchange our last set of notes. Our goodbyes. Within a few minutes of reading her note, I'm choking on tears and gasping for air, embarrassed by my inability to control myself. All the goodbyes have caught up with me. Thankfully I'm at school and not at home, where Mom would likely criticize me for being too emotional––something she always says when I cry.

Mom's plan is to fly to Virginia by herself so that she can set up our temporary apartment while Rascal and I stay with my uncle, aunt, and cousins. The plan is for me to follow behind in a few days, flying to Virginia, with Rascal, on my own. Since I've flown by myself so many times, I'm not too worried. Although five hours on a plane sounds like a lot.

My cousin Marisa shares her room with us. That first night, Rascal whines and howls for hours, pacing the walled perimeter, jumping on and off the bed, confused and agitated. I worry about how upset he is, and that his noise might be keeping everyone awake. But I don't know how to calm or comfort him. I sneak downstairs to put him in the garage, so at least his cries won't bother the others. Since he's largely an outdoor cat, he should be safe out there.

When I wake up in the morning, I creep downstairs to check on him, but he's nowhere to be found. Scanning the garage side to side, I notice a rectangular hole near the base of the wall. The grate that once covered it lays on the ground. Rascal must have pushed it aside and gotten out. I run outside calling for him. Who knows what time he escaped. He may have been gone for hours by now. But where would he go?

My stomach lurches. The earth slides away and my ears buzz. I step back to steady myself and sit on the steps. Rascal's been with me day after day, year after year. A constant presence. I don't even remember life before Rascal.

I want to run back to my old house, crawl into bed, throw my arms around Bear, and cry. Let it all out. All the sorrow from the many leavings. But I don't. Instead, I hide my feelings. It's what I usually do now to protect myself from being criticized for being too emotional. For the next day and a half, I tuck myself into the bathroom and cry into the towels, careful not to make much noise. I don't want to trouble my aunt and uncle or my cousins, so I act as if losing Rascal is not the leveling experience that it is. When I'm not hiding and weeping, I walk around the block hunting for Rascal and calling his name. My younger cousins follow closely behind calling his name too. But time is running out.

By Saturday, I'm on a plane, knowing I'll never see Rascal again.

Chapter 8

Monday morning, I'm in my first class at Longfellow Middle School in McLean, Virginia, still bleary-eyed from the time-zone change and reeling from the many goodbyes. But I can't think about that right now. There are seismic changes to navigate—the clothing, the cliques, the haircuts, the slang, the "y'alls," the weather. Everything about this Southern state is vastly different from Northern California. Is there a fast track to fitting in here? I'm going to have to find out.

While the adjustment to school and life in a new state goes fairly well at first, everything worsens between Mom and me. Within a few months, she begins dating another Tom, who has a young and annoying seven-year-old son named Will. I barely acknowledge them and stick my tongue out at Will when no one's looking.

Throughout the entire first summer, the four of us go to concerts at Wolftrap Farm Park and to museums in downtown DC. It's the Bicentennial. Mom says there's so much to see and do and learn, but I hate being dragged around and having people think we might be a real family. Why won't she leave me home alone like she's always done? Why does she want me with her now? And who the hell cares about First Lady dresses and dinosaur bones?

One morning she's adamant we go––yet *again*––to the Museum of Natural History. When I huff and puff in resistance, she says she doesn't like my attitude.

"You're just like your father."

Knowing how much she dislikes Dad, the comment surprises me. Is this her ultimate insult? Maybe. Although I'm not sure what she means exactly. What does she see in me that reminds her of what she hates about him? Of course, I don't ask. It doesn't matter. Since I don't want to be anything like her, being like Dad sounds like a good thing. The comment fuels my motivation to dig in harder against her plans for another day of museums. Finally, she relents and storms out of the house, driving off to meet Tom and Will.

I'm relieved and exhausted. There's no reprieve from her. What if there were though? What if I could move back to California? Maybe I don't have to stay here.

That night, I phone Dad and beg to come live with him. His voice is calm and reassuring. "Sure, hon. That would be great. I'll need to work things out with your mom. I'll call you tomorrow, and we can figure out the details."

The next day, I pace my bedroom waiting for his call, checking the time on my AM/FM radio alarm clock, careful to calculate the three-hour time difference.

I'm giddy at the prospect of getting away from her. Of not having to be subject to her demands and fits of anger. I'm also excited to live closer to Carolyn and Kerry. I've missed them so much. Why haven't I thought of this sooner? It's really the perfect solution to all my problems.

But Dad doesn't call. I wait the next day too. The giddiness subsides, even though my hopes remain strong. Several days slide by without a call. Then weeks pass.

Something in me resists calling him again. I've already begged, desperately asking for what I want and need. My requests have been met with silence. That stings.

Finally, I break down and call again. The urgency from weeks ago has subsided, but I still want out. The phone doesn't even ring. Instead, there are screeching chime sounds followed by a recording, which states that the number I have dialed has been disconnected. *Disconnected?* How can that be? He's vanished? And completely abandoned me?

Did my pleas push him over the edge? Did he disappear because of me? Is it the drinking? Did everything become too much to handle? The divorce.

Losing the big house. Having me whine and beg to be cared for. Maybe he just couldn't take it anymore.

Maybe there's something about me that's difficult to love, difficult to stick around for. In the absence of facts and unable to explain the unexplainable, I assume it's me. It must be my fault. But I also blame the alcohol. If he's an alcoholic who's drinking too much, he must not be in his right mind. That would explain why he's doing things that seem out of character. Because what other explanation could there be?

• • •

With all escape routes from Mom closed tight, there's no place of refuge. I'm trapped. I have no voice. No power. No way to change my circumstances. And she's right about one thing: I have a bad attitude.

I've also come to some conclusions. Whether I follow her rules makes no difference. She's going to be mad no matter what. But for now, at least, she's not seeing Tom anymore and no longer trying to pretend we're a happy family of four. She's back to leaving me at home alone and not dragging me to museums.

As I enter ninth grade, the tight leash she's tried to contain me with is off. Not because she's relaxed the rules, but because I discovered how to chew through the harness to set myself free.

Rules and leashes be damned. I sneak out at night. I drink. I'm rarely home by curfew. And I lie—all the time.

One evening, she confronts me with information she heard from a colleague. "Joe saw you hitchhiking on Kirby road."

"No, that wasn't me."

"I know it was you. He knew it was you."

"It wasn't."

"Oh, really?" she says, mocking me.

"Yes, really," I parrot back.

"You were wearing that shirt with your name on it: KIM. That wasn't you?" she asks, describing my cute periwinkle-blue T-shirt with three floral fabric letters embroidered across the chest that I wore two days earlier.

"No! It wasn't me. I don't know who he saw. But it wasn't me."

Even in the face of strong evidence, I commit to the lie, rooting my feet where I stand and squaring my shoulders in defiance. She stomps off, exasperated and shaking her head.

Mom says I can't be trusted. I think her reaction to everything is the problem. I also think it's unfair of her to want it both ways. She's always wanted freedom from *and* control over me. For years, she's been largely absent and unavailable, living life on her own terms. Yet she wants to control everything I do through rules and intimidation.

She has long believed I should know right from wrong and choose appropriately in all situations, with no adult guidance or supervision required. In my mind, she doesn't want to be bothered. She wants to parent from afar. Or have me parent myself.

Do as I say, not as I do creates a quandary. Do I grow up to be like her or grow up to be the person I've been told to be? What becomes of the person who must raise herself?

Am I to become an independent freethinker? A woman with her own mind and ambition? That's going to require standing up to Mom, going against her. Or am I to become a fearful and compliant rule follower? The one who falls in line with what she and everyone else wants? A path of utter compliance to rules and demands. With such mixed messages, it's difficult to know who I am becoming. Or who I *should* become.

Being unleashed doesn't add up to unfettered freedom. Instead, bucking the rules––and consequently, getting caught––means I spend nearly the entire first half of ninth grade being punished. As soon as I get off restriction and am free to go out again, I'm back in trouble once more.

A month after I turn fourteen in November and before I am of legal age for a work permit, I land a job at a shoe store at the local mall. I lied about my age. I figure having a job is an ideal way to get out of the house and away from Mom. She respects work, so I assume she won't stop me from going to work even when I'm forbidden to leave the house. So, if I lose phone privileges, I can still see my friends while they're hanging out at the mall. They can join me for a cigarette break.

• • •

Since moving to Virginia, I've navigated my way through a series of different friend groups, incorporating the lessons I learned in elementary school, at camp, and in junior high. I've honed my ability to keep their questions of "Why?" at bay. I do most of the asking, discovering much more about others than they do about me. This approach protects me. If I haven't opened up, they can ditch me as a friend without prompting the sting of betrayal. Plus, asking questions is a road to fitting in. When people sense you're interested in them, they willingly talk about themselves and are more inclined to like you.

One Saturday night, my friends and I go to a party near Occoquan, miles from our homes. I tell Mom I'm staying at Pam's house, but we all crash on the floor and sprawl across couches at the home where the party's held. A loud, hard knock at the door jolts us awake at two o'clock in the morning. My friend's father has tracked us down and marches us to his car for the long drive back to McLean. I'm going to be in big trouble. The closer we get to my house, the more afraid I become.

I turn the doorknob slowly. Maybe I can creep up to my room before she sees me. I push the door lightly before it suddenly bursts open. Mom stands in front of me in her bathrobe. Black streaks of mascara stain her cheeks. She's been crying. The sight stuns me for a moment. I've rarely seen her like this. And why is she crying? Is she actually upset that something happened to me? Was she worried about me?

Before I can say a word, she launches a strong backhand to my face, landing hard and square across my cheek. It knocks me sideways.

"Where the hell have you been?"

My first inclination is to lie. But that would be pointless. I tell her details she already knows, standing in the foyer with my face burning, head hanging low.

"Go to your room, young lady," she commands. "I have a lot of thinking to do."

She doesn't dole out a punishment on the spot as she usually does. I retreat to my room wondering what's going to happen.

What options do I have? Maybe she'll send me to boarding school. That's a good idea. I'd get out of this house. She'd be rid of me. I decide to lobby for that option.

The next morning, she announces that I'm going to a different school. A private school away from all the friends influencing me. I beg to go to boarding school instead.

"I don't want to send you away. We have only a few years left together before you head off to college," she says.

I puzzle over her response. Based on her actions, she's never wanted me around—unless you count the Tom and Will phase, which I don't. Why keep me here now?

The answer doesn't matter. She's made her decision. What Mom wants, Mom gets.

The very next day, I'm a new freshman at Flint Hill Prep, a small private school in the neighboring town. Since I'm only fourteen and unable to drive, I have to ride the short yellow bus to school—the most uncool mode of transportation ever. Each day, I slink low behind the seats as we wind our way through the streets of McLean, hoping no one will recognize me. It's mortifying to ride that damn bus.

At Flint Hill, there are two types of students: those who've attended since kindergarten and those who've been ripped from their public schools because they're getting in too much trouble. This second group of kids are far more advanced in their sex, drugs, and rock 'n' roll ways than any of my friends in McLean. If Mom only knew what her hard-earned dollars are exposing me to now.

• • •

In bed one night, I realize I've left a letter to my neighbor from California on the end table in the family room. In it, I've shared explicit details of life that week. Panicked, I climb out of bed and down the stairs.

Mom is out with Russ, her latest boyfriend. Are they home yet? She must be home; I turned those lights off before going upstairs. Had I not, she would've woken me up from a sound sleep and made me go downstairs to turn them off myself. She'd never do me the favor of turning them off, instead always leaning into teaching me a lesson.

Maybe she's watching TV or reading.

The mottled white, brown, and orange shag carpet crunches beneath my toes. I turn the corner to find her sitting in the chair beside the end table, letter in hand. She looks up, then back down, and proceeds to read it.

"Dear, Gina. Holy shit, have I got news to tell you." Her voice is thick with sarcasm.

"Stop!" I shout, throwing myself at her and trying to grab the letter from her hands.

She pushes me hard. I stumble, trip over my feet, and fall square on my butt. Then she comes for me. I crabwalk backward. She lunges for my shoulders. I kick hard with my right foot, trying to get her to back off. She grabs my foot in midair, both hands firmly around my ankle, and walks backward. Pulling with all her might, she drags me across the carpet, my left leg folding beneath me. I recline back, twisting my trunk to find something to grab on to. The carpet burns my shin.

"Stop!" I scream, kicking wildly with my right leg, hoping to shake loose of her grip. One kick lands in her gut, forcing her to let go. She clutches her stomach.

I can't believe we're brawling in the family room. Huffing, puffing, and staring at each other, we seem to recognize at the exact same moment that I am no longer seven or eight or twelve. No longer unable or unwilling to fight back. I'm defending myself.

At an impasse, she picks the letter off the floor, crumbles it into a ball, throws it into the kitchen trash, and stomps off to her bedroom. She doesn't speak to me for three days.

Chapter 9

The first time I see Willy, he's driving a baby-blue Pontiac. The muffler rumbles as he slows to a stop in front of the house where my friends and I are partying. He hangs one arm outside the driver's-side window, a cigarette dangling from his lips.

My friend Ben approaches the car, puts his left hand on the rooftop, and leans in low. They talk for several minutes. I watch, drawing long, slow drags off my cigarette. As Ben turns to walk away, Willy's eyes catch mine. He breaks into a sly smile, nods his head, and drives away, giving the accelerator an extra pump so that the muffler roars again.

I see him several more times over the next few weeks at parties and Ben's house. He lights my cigarettes and asks for my phone number. I've had crushes and dates and puppy-love boyfriends, but no relationship that's lasted longer than a month or two.

It's May 1977, the end of freshman year. Led Zeppelin—the world's greatest band—is playing at the Capital Center. But I don't have tickets.

The night of the concert, I awake to a soft tapping on my window. I sit up and pull back the sheer yellow curtains to look down from my second-story window. Willy is standing on the deck below, throwing small rocks to get my attention. A Led Zeppelin T-shirt is fanned out on the chair in front of him.

"Hey," he whispers.

"What are you doing?" I smile. How did he even know where I lived or which room was mine?

"I know you wanted to go to the concert, so I bought you a shirt." He looks down at the black concert T-shirt, emblazoned with a naked Robert Plant in a giant pair of wings leaping into the air, back arched and arms outstretched.

"Oh my god, thank you! Thank you. I love it. But I can't come down right now."

"It's okay. I know," he smiles and waves goodbye, his lanky frame slinking back into the darkness.

I sit in bed for several minutes until I'm confident Mom is sleeping and Willy is gone. I sneak downstairs to retrieve the T-shirt, holding it open, then pulling it to my chest and hugging it tightly.

I can't believe he did that. I tiptoe back upstairs. There are those tweety birds and dancing hearts. I rerun the scene in my head: pulling back the curtain, seeing him grinning on the deck, the shirt splayed out on the chair. It's as perfect and romantic a moment as in the movies.

That's how Willy and I begin dating.

From the start, Mom doesn't like him. She hates that he waits in the car and honks for me to come out. He never comes to the door, she says. But I don't want him coming to the door because she would just embarrass me, calling me Kimmy or reminding him of my curfew. And he has little interest in talking with adults. It's best to keep them as far apart as possible.

Our relationship is intense. All-consuming. He's in my thoughts when I'm in class. When I'm at work. When I'm with friends. But it's not just my mind that's obsessed; my body is too. We have long make-out sessions wherever we are. In his car, in my basement, in open fields. Our legs tangle together, our bodies so close, no daylight shines between us.

He's the first boy I fall in love with, and I fall hard. When we have sex for the first time, I'm nervous. More than anything, I want him to love me. Forever. And never leave me.

Because I wasn't raised with religion or notions of purity and sin, I have no qualms about losing my virginity. If anything, Mom has counseled me to have premarital sex, saying, "You have to know what you're getting into." That's better than being a virgin on your wedding night, she explains.

In the women's liberation era, having sex has become a marker of equality. Women can be just like men, have sex with whomever we want without any downsides or repercussions. Can't we? So, I expected to have sex before I got married, although I didn't necessarily think it would happen when I was fourteen years old.

Willy can't get enough of me. And he doesn't want to share me with anyone. He picks me up from school when he doesn't have to work so that I don't have to ride the stupid little yellow bus. He surprises me at work and hangs out on the bench in front of the store until my break. I love the attention.

He makes it clear that he doesn't want me talking to other guys. Which is fine. I'm not interested in other guys, so I don't mind following his rules. I'm used to rules. Yet early on in our relationship, I notice he's quick to anger, even when there isn't anything to be mad about. In some ways, he reminds me of Mom.

In August, four months into dating, I go to Ocean City, Maryland, for a week with a friend and her family. They've rented a beach house on Third Street, near the base of the boardwalk.

"Why do you hang out with her? She's a total slut," Willy says.

"She is not. I like her." And I do. Terri hasn't had an easy home life. We have a lot in common. Most kids are afraid of her, ever since she got into a fistfight in seventh grade. But we get along well.

"Her reputation is going to rub off on you."

"Why is that? Why can't mine rub off on her?" I ask. He doesn't answer.

At the beach, Terri and I spend our days lying on the sand, playing Crazy Eights at the kitchen table, and walking up and down the boardwalk. One evening, we linger near the carnival rides while she flirts with a skater boy from Maryland.

We walk to our favorite arcade, then to get ice cream. When we stop, I spot Willy. He and a group of friends are ten paces behind us.

I'm confused. What is he doing here? My heart quickens. Blood sinks to my feet. Have they been following us? Even though I haven't done anything wrong, panic rises. I don't want him mad at me. Or for us to break up. Did he see us talking to those guys?

I sidle up to him as if I haven't a worry in the world.

"Oh my gosh! What are you guys doing here?" I squeal and smile, hoping to show how happy I am to see him, to cajole him away from anger.

"Oh, nothin'," he says, nodding his head up and down. He thinks he's caught me. I can sense it in his stance, in his eyes.

"I'm so glad," I purr, going in for a hug, wrapping my arms around his waist and placing my head against his chest.

"What have you been up to?" he asks.

"Nothing, just hanging out."

"Uh-huh"

I pull away and step back. "We're just going to get ice cream. Do you guys want to come?" I ask, addressing his gang of friends. They nod. I grab his hand and pull him toward the ice cream shack.

After a moment, he says, "We were following you for a while."

"Why didn't you just tell me you were here."

"Just wanted to see what you were up to."

"As you saw, not much." I force my voice to steady. I don't want him to think he's caught me doing something wrong. Because he hasn't.

• • •

Willy's rigid rules, mistrust, and anger are all too familiar. Rules and rebuke are what I know best. So, when our relationship devolves from here into a rhythm of volatile arguments, I hardly notice. We swing frenetically between sex and strife. We fight, break up, then slam back together days later.

Eight months into this cycle, I grow weary. With him. With what we have. I love the idea of being loved. But not if this is what love entails.

One afternoon, while Mom is at work, he and I argue in the foyer of our house, my back to the stairwell, my head against the vertical wooden banister. He's furious with me. In that moment, I don't care. I'm tired of trying to please and appease. Of always having to do what someone else tells me to do. Of always having someone mad at me.

I stand defiantly, glaring at him. He balls his fist, steps closer, one foot forward, and yells in my face.

I dare you. Hit me, I think to myself.

Being hit is my threshold. That's where I'll draw the line. It's as if I want him to hit me, so I can have a concrete reason to end the relationship. It's not enough to no longer *want* to be with him. Because I don't think he'll accept that; and I don't have the courage to leave otherwise. His fist whizzes past my left ear and crashes into the banister.

Before today, our volatility—the yelling, anger, and tension—felt familiar. I know rage and ugliness. It doesn't unmoor me. But seeing him, hearing him punch the banister, pushes me past the limits of what I'm willing to accept. I don't want the edge of what I'll tolerate to slide, tricking me into becoming accustomed to even worse treatment than I'm already used to.

Aren't I hoping to become an independent woman who takes care of and stands up for herself? This moment is a warning sign. Because it's only a matter of time before that punch lands in my face.

Willy rubs his knuckles. I step away from the banister and walk to the front door, opening it wide.

"My mom's going to be home soon. You should probably go." The mention of Mom is startling, even to me. What would she have done had she found me bloodied and bruised upon her return from work? How would I explain what happened? My chest tightens. There's a sting of tears, though I don't want to cry.

"Just go," I implore.

He shakes his head and walks out. The car muffler roars in the distance.

How will I ever find a life of quiet and calm if I surround myself with people who are hot-tempered and explosive?

Chapter 10

During sophomore year in 1978, a couple of months after Willy and I break up, the DC area is hit with a large snowstorm. Schools are canceled for Friday, so I spend Thursday night at Pam's house. We trudge in the snow to a party at Kiki and her brother Mike's house, a half-mile down the road. They're from my old school, the public one Mom took me out of. Kiki's a year older than Pam and me, and I've had a crush on Mike since freshman year. Twenty or so people gather by the keg in the kitchen, where Pam and I stand talking to Kiki.

Toward the end of the night, Mike approaches. We've never spoken before. He bounces in his shoes as he talks, raking his jet-black hair with his left hand, leaving it in rows of soft waves that cascade over his forehead and curl around his ears. He's wearing jeans, Timberland boots, and an untucked red flannel shirt.

After an hour or so, he asks, "Want to check out the basement?"

"Sure."

He leads me downstairs to the rec room. Pasted to the cinder-block walls are album covers. Pink Floyd. The Who. Little Feat. A poster of Farrah Fawcett smiling, chin up, hand behind her mane of curls, donning a red bathing suit.

A large bed is pushed up against one wall beneath a small casement window. It's topped with piles of pillows in different shapes and sizes. They disguise rumpled sheets and a bedspread.

"Here, sit," he says, plopping down on the bed.

He kisses me slowly. We make out for several minutes, shifting our weight to lay down awkwardly amid the pillows. He pushes some aside to make more room. I still have my boots on, so I angle myself to keep them off the bed.

I can't believe he's kissing me. Mike!

We fumble and roll for several minutes. I mimic the motions I've watched in movies. My right arm loops around his shoulder; the fingers on my left hand tangle in his curls and rub his scalp. I pull his face closer to mine, opening my mouth wide. We clink teeth as he presses his mouth harder into mine.

He sits up on his knees and reaches for my zipper.

"No, no," I whisper, grabbing his hand gently and pushing it away.

He lays down on top of me, wriggles his arm and hand between us, and tries again, pinning me against the bed. He manages to unfasten the button of my jeans.

"No," I repeat.

"Come on," he says, grabbing the zipper pull with a tug.

"No, no," I say a bit more firmly. It's way too soon. I'm just getting to know him.

He ignores my pleas and sits up, unzips my pants, and uses both hands to yank them down. I struggle against him, twisting my hips to try to keep my pants on. Even though he is thin and scrawny, he is much stronger than me. Fighting him physically doesn't seem like an option. I'm frozen, unsure of what is happening.

"Please don't," I say, hot tears spilling from the corners of my eyes.

He doesn't say another word as he pushes my underwear down and wedges himself between my legs. I continue to plead, asking him to stop. His bony hips thrust hard against the inside of my thighs. I cry, but I don't scream. I don't hit. I don't flail. I just want to get through this moment as quickly as I can.

I hear a small group of people lingering upstairs. I wonder if they can hear me. If so, why aren't they coming to help?

How is this boy I've had a crush on for so long treating me like this? How is he having sex with me, ignoring my pleas to stop? What is wrong with him?

He thrusts for what seems an eternity. I have no idea how long, but my legs recoil from the force, as if someone is taking a baseball bat to the soft, fleshy part of my upper thighs.

When he's done, he lays there, breathing into my left ear. I can smell nicotine on his breath and hear the dryness of his mouth, the sticky sound of a tongue with no saliva. He pushes himself up on one arm, rolls over, sits up, throws on his jeans, and bounces upstairs, he says, to get some water.

I sit up too, my feet still dangling off the edge of the bed, my boots still on. I stand slowly. It hurts to bend down to grab my underwear, which twists around my shins like a ligature. I unroll them and pull them up, then wince as I pull up my jeans.

He returns, bounding down the stairs like a puppy.

"Pam's gone. Most everyone is. There's a lot of snow out there. Why don't you stay here for the night, and I'll walk you back to Pam's in the morning."

I'm so confused by everything that's just happened. I don't have it in me to walk to Pam's in the middle of the night by myself. I don't even know what time it is. I nod and lay back down on the bed, on my side, facing away from him. My body throbs. I can tell my face is caked with crusted tears and melted mascara.

I don't sleep, anxious for the morning to come, so I can walk back to Pam's. I replay the scene again and again in my head. How did this happen? What did I do wrong? Did I land in this situation because I'm so desperate for love and attention? I can't believe I thought I liked this guy.

When he wakes up, he's perky.

"Do you want to walk up to get breakfast at the Sunrise Diner?" he asks.

He wants to have a breakfast date? Doesn't he know what he did?

"No, thanks," I whisper. "I need to get back home. I'll just walk from here."

I want to get away, but I don't want to make a scene. As hurt as I am, I still want him to like me. Or rather, I don't want him to dislike me.

When my ultimate goal is to be liked, or to fit in, it seems I'm willing to sacrifice nearly everything for that pursuit. I grab my coat from upstairs and make my way back to Pam's house. I'm not ready to go home. I need more time to think.

I tell Pam bits and pieces from the night but am too shaken to share specifics. She tells me people heard me crying. I'm embarrassed and disappointed to learn my supposed friends overheard what was happening and did nothing to help.

About an hour later, I leave Pam's and head home; a walk which normally takes twenty minutes takes twice as long. Every step requires extra effort because of the eight inches of snow blanketing the ground and the fact that my legs are as unsteady as a newborn foal's.

The sun is blinding. The sky is the kind of bright blue that should be allowed only on happy days. I want to blink the world away.

As I approach the house, I see Mom shoveling the driveway. I lower my head, barely acknowledging her as I enter the garage, take off my boots, and walk gingerly to my room. I peel off my clothes so that I can shower. Everything burns. My crotch. My thighs. Even my feet hurt.

Tears mingle with warm water. I turn my back to the shower head; the water slides down my back. Can I wash it all away? The posters. The keg beer. His nonchalance. My pleas to stop.

Replaying every moment bakes the night into memory. I feel scorched. Like a tree whose bark is charred by fire. And also like a tree, I'm still standing. Because trees do that, don't they? As long as their roots aren't burned, they can survive fire. I've seen countless trees, especially California redwoods, seared and standing. They look beat up, but then they resprout. It's how they've thrived for millions of years.

The hot water runs out, and the cold snaps me out of the trance. I turn the handles and grab a towel, gently rubbing myself dry. Deep scarlet bruises line both thighs. They're tender to the touch. Even the towel's small terry cloth nubs are too abrasive, like sandpaper on my swollen skin. I've never experienced anything like this. Never seen bruises this big. Never felt this sore all over. I can't even pee without pain.

The bruises worsen throughout the weekend, turning from scarlet to dark purple. I rub my fingers over them lightly and cry some more. I can't stop crying.

Mom realizes something's wrong. She asks me repeatedly what's the matter.

I lie, saying, "Nothing. I just miss my old school." It's been a common complaint of mine for months. I don't consider telling her what happened, assuming she'd blame or punish me like she always does.

On Saturday evening, Mom calls me for dinner. The antique oak dining chairs are hard and unforgiving, like everything around me. I look at my plate, my bangs sheltering my eyes and emotions, and don't say a word.

"I've made a decision," she declares. "I've decided you can go back to McLean, starting Monday. It's not worth having you be so miserable."

I raise my head and stare at her. After all this time, I'm getting exactly what I've wanted: the ability to return to my old school and all my friends. Given what just happened with Mike, the timing couldn't be worse.

"Thank you," I sniff half-heartedly, trying to show enthusiasm. "Thank you."

"You're welcome."

On Monday, I re-enroll in McLean High School and worry that everyone is talking about me and Mike. I decide to avoid the smoking court, preferring to steer clear of him and my old friends—the ones who failed to come to my rescue—until I can be sure any rumors have died down.

Once again, it seems I need to make new friends.

Chapter 11

During the year at Flint Hill, most of my McLean High friends either became pregnant, dropped out, or were forced to change schools like I was. Even if Mike hadn't done what he did, I would've needed a new gang eventually.

Five schools in five years has taught me how to make friends while trying to protect myself from the risk of betrayal, abandonment, and general disinterest. I've also learned to be cautious; it's easier to engage others than to reveal much of myself. The art of asking questions means the focus isn't on me.

Blending in, being absorbed into a crowd or clique, is easiest that way. Most people don't begrudge a place in the pack if they get to talk about themselves. Given the chance to confide, they do——often mistaking the exchange for intimacy. They rarely pose their own questions. After years studying the room, I can echo its mood and very nearly disappear in plain sight. Keeping people at a safe distance, I tell myself, means less heartache or disappointment for me.

This time, switching schools is simpler. Not everyone's a stranger; I know many faces from past classes or hallways. My stay-under-the-radar approach works again. I end up knowing more about my friends' lives than they ever learn about mine. Partly because no one asks and partly because I'm skilled at steering away conversations.

As I change colors to adjust to whatever people seem to want, my demeanor also shifts—soft-spoken one moment, giggly the next. With sharp listening and good memory, I'm everyone's sounding board. When a friend worries about a boy or a problem at home, I follow up the next day: *Did Rob ask you out? Was your mom mad?* Not to be nosy but to show interest. To confirm I'm worth having around. My grades might be awful, but I excel at emotional intelligence.

Despite building a wide circle of friends, I'm still searching for someone to replace Renee. Someone who can be a trusted confidante. I crave deep, intimate connections—I just don't want to be destroyed if they end.

How do we live with such opposing goals? How do we protect our hearts and still allow them to love?

My habit of asking questions becomes a litmus test as I hunt for others who will reciprocate. Only those who show genuine curiosity about me and my life earn my trust. Few clear that bar. But when someone does, my walls crumble fast.

Over time, I come to love a handful of friends—*true* friends like Renee was—who begin to fill the holes left by family and loneliness like sap sealing the cracks of a wounded tree. Their steady presence fortifies me; their desire to know the *real* me, not the chameleon version of me, is a salve.

• • •

It's been years since I've heard from Dad. Birthdays pass unnoticed. It seems unfathomable: to have a child and completely ignore them. Does he even remember my birthday?

Carolyn still sends cards with pictures of Kerry, though she's remarried now, with three new stepdaughters. No one talks about me visiting anymore, and I don't bring it up.

Just before junior year, a card arrives from Dad. Maybe he's doing better now, or well enough to be in touch more consistently. After stints in California and Texas, he's settled in Florida. Even after reading the card, which provides little information other than the fact that he's moved and alive, I don't know if he's working or still drinking. Despite how he up and left with no notice, I jump at the chance to write him back, hoping once again that things can be different between us. I tread lightly in my reply—sharing minimal details, glossing over life at home, brimming with enthusiasm—because I'm afraid my previous pleas to live with him scared him away. Maybe his silence was my fault.

I include no signs in the letter that I *need* him because neediness might cause him run again. Quite the opposite. I want to offer reasons to stay, as if whispering, *Don't you want to witness this, be part of it all?*

• • •

Midyear, I start dating Brian. I'm turned inside out by him. The honey-golden hair that falls softly to his shoulders, the twinkle of his eyes, his ever-present grin. He's by far the cutest boy I've ever dated. One afternoon, he drops me at the mall for my shift. A tender goodbye turns into a full make-out session in the back of his forest-green Ford Bronco, and I skip work altogether, later blaming a flat tire.

Normally I'm dependable, proud of my work ethic. My job is the one place I feel capable and confident. The lie shakes me. Even though I'm never found out, I know I've let down my manager. It's not who I want to be or how I want to act.

Lying to Mom, however, doesn't spark such guilt. Her constant disappointment and anger are now simply the unavoidable thorns in the briar patch of our relationship. No matter how carefully I move, her moods still cut and draw blood.

People talk about walking on eggshells, but volatility at home is more like standing at a gun range with shots ringing out in deafening succession. Initially, even when you know the sounds are coming, you flinch, until finally your body and brain learn to go numb and not react.

That's how it is for me now: I'm numb at home.

Kind people—like my store manager—show what life can be like elsewhere: calm, predictable, light. I'd do anything to preserve that, to have that be my every day.

A few months later, after writing Brian's English essay for him so that he can graduate, he breaks up with me while we sit in his truck at the top of my driveway. I knew it was coming—he'd been flirting with Robin—but still, I'm gutted. I collect my things, step out, and stand small beside the massive green truck. When he drives away, I dissolve into tears.

Mom finds me crying on the bed.

"Brian broke up with me," I whisper, hoping for comfort.

"Oh. Well, men are like buses. There's always another one around the corner. You'll be fine," she says, patting my leg before leaving.

Of course she'd say that. I roll over and turn up *Desperado*, the perfect soundtrack for endless weeping.

In the shower a few days later, I notice a strange habit: I talk to myself—not really *to* myself, but to my imagined future children. It's a wiser parental version of me, saying everything I wish I'd heard growing up. Advice on friends, love, and honesty. And now, on heartbreak and losing someone you think you love.

The pain of rejection will fade, even if it lingers when you see them again.

Lying might seem easier, but it erodes trust.

Sleeping with someone won't make you feel loved.

These fictitious conversations become my compass. In the absence of guidance, I parent myself one pep talk at a time.

● ● ●

Mom's baseline fury confounds me. She has everything she could want—a beautiful home, an exciting job, friends, money, travel. Why so angry? More specifically, why so angry with me?

At home, she's perfected two voices. Terse and hard-edged with me, soft and doughy with others. One minute barking orders around the house, then answering the phone with a syrupy, "Oh, hiiii!"

The contrast infuriates me. Shouldn't you treat family better than you treat others? At the same time, seeing the shift is a reminder that there are other sides to her.

Typically, we have little to talk about and she rarely listens when I speak. Her eyes glaze over; her mind drifts. Once I notice these signs, I retreat, refusing to chase her attention.

Yet I search for the moments when she softens around me, like on Sunday mornings and during meals out. When she's almost pleasant and more willing to be present.

"I'm starting to think about college," I say one Sunday morning.

"Well, you'll need to get your grades up, but I'm glad you're putting your mind to it," she replies, stabbing her eggs.

"I know. I'm trying."

"Let's hope it's not too little, too late. What will you study?"

She's still engaged, so I keep going. "I think communications. Maybe broadcast journalism."

"Mm-hmm." Her eyes flick toward my plate. "Do you really need more hash browns?"

"Yes," I say, rolling my eyes. "I'm thinking of Boulder or Tampa. Both have strong programs."

"Okay. Good for you."

Both schools are also far from Virginia, though I don't mention that part. Putting distance between us is the point. College is my road out.

• • •

By fall of my senior year of high school in 1979, Mom travels often for work, leaving me home for weeks at a time.

"It's good practice for when you're on your own," she says.

Which is fine by me. I love the house when it's quiet. Light pours through the back windows, and the garden explodes with tulips, azaleas, and phlox. I sit on the deck beneath the oak tree, smoking, admiring ribbons of color. Nowhere is as beautiful as Virginia in springtime, and our backyard might be the most beautiful spot of all.

Alone, I feel completely at ease. Still, I like the company of friends who come and go, sleeping over when they can. We're not wild. I still go to school and to work, maintaining a steady routine. Freedom itself is enough. The peace feels like luxury.

• • •

By early spring, when college acceptance letters begin arriving, I race to the mailbox.

We regret to inform you…

Again and again. Each letter stings. Boulder. Florida. Tampa. Georgia. All rejections.

"Well, that's what you get," Mom scolds. "I told you to get your grades up."

Panic sets in. My ability to escape home vaporizes before my eyes. What now? I scour *Barron's Profile of American Colleges* for schools that accept anyone, sending out a second wave of applications.

Finally: *We are pleased to accept you to the University of North Carolina at Wilmington.*

It's official! I'm going to college. I'm getting out. Six and a half hours away by car, five miles from the beach. August can't come fast enough.

• • •

By now, solitude feels natural. Yet sometimes, when Mom stays out late at night, I'm gripped by fears that haven't plagued me before. Lying awake, I consider what would happen if she doesn't come back. What if she died tonight? Who would take me? Would I be shipped to California before graduation? Would all my plans disintegrate overnight?

So close to freedom yet not quite there. The thought squeezes my lungs until I hear her key in the door. Relief, then dread, knowing it might return the next time she's late.

• • •

The week of graduation, a card arrives from Dad—signed *Larry and Joyce.* I stare at it. Married? Without telling me?

Apparently, I have a new stepmother to add to the growing count: one biological mother, two stepmothers, one biological father, one ex-adoptive father, one step-stepfather. Apart from Mom, none of them are really in my life. They've all but vanished.

Still, finding out about this news in this way hurts. The card is proof of the distance between us. And I notice, for the first time, that he signs his name *Larry.* Somewhere along the way, he stopped being "Dad," and I hadn't even realized it.

Chapter 12

In late summer of 1980, I head off to the University of North Carolina at Wilmington—UNCW. I relish being away and on my own, soaking up the culture that reigns in the coastal plain and tidewater region of North Carolina, where Wilmington sits on the Cape Fear River. Within the first few weeks of school, I receive a letter from Mom, which makes me weep.

She says she's proud of me. She encourages me to make the most of my time at college, to work hard, and to get good grades. She closes with a plea to realize that this is the best time of my life. They are the kindest words she has ever shared with me.

I'm buoyed. Perhaps we've reached a turning point. Maybe now that I'm stepping into adulthood and independence, we can shed the tension between us. If she's not worrying about raising me, maybe she'll be less angry. If we're on more equal footing, maybe we can build a better, more loving relationship. I'm as hopeful as I am naïve.

During my first semester, I find close friends on my hall. I'm introduced to pig pickings and hush puppies, beach music and its jitterbug-like dance, the shag. I learn to say "hey" instead of "hi," and to "mash" the light switch instead of turning it off. Within a few months, when I'm out drinking at night, I slur with a Southern drawl. I also take school seriously, diving into my studies and managing a 3.0 average the first semester.

But college isn't all easy and breezy. Too many nights, I fall into bed in a drunken stupor, pinned to the mattress by Tilt-A-Whirl bed spins that make me so nauseous that I throw up in the trash can on the floor.

It's in this hazy blur of hungover mornings when my friends and I reek of alcohol that I first smell it. A scent long ago deposited in the bank of childhood memories that suddenly spills forth, like pennies clanking onto a table. That sweet, tangy smell that made my nose wiggle each time I hugged Dad. It was the smell of a grown-up party. More specifically, it was stale, day-old alcohol fermenting and seeping from his pores.

The realization hits hard. Not only was Dad drinking, but he must've been binging. No one I know reeks after just a few beers. All those visits, all those adventures, he was either wasted or hungover.

I think back to how I learned the news about him and Carolyn divorcing. About how much time I spent with her but not necessarily with him. About the stories of rehab and bottles behind toilets. How she coordinated my visits and cared for me.

All those years, she'd kept up a façade. They weren't like the happily married couples I'd watched on TV. Without Carolyn propping him up, perhaps his life unraveled. Maybe his disappearance had nothing to do with me or my pleas. It was alcoholism.

I am both stunned and sympathetic, quick to forgive. Because if alcohol wasn't involved, maybe he would've been a great dad. Perhaps he would've rescued me from living with Mom after all.

• • •

Midway through freshman year, my roommate and I meet a group of guys who live on the second floor of the dorm next door. They're all at least a year ahead of us. Steve is the ringleader. He's big. In every way. His body, his laugh, his presence. He knows how to command a room.

He's not my type. I'm not sure I have a type, but if I did, it wouldn't be Steve—with his ruddy cheeks, pasty skin, linebacker build, man-boobs, and clammy hands. He constantly swipes the sweat from his upper lip with his index finger whenever it beads on his peach-fuzz mustache. He wheezes when he laughs and waddles when he walks.

No, he's definitely not my type. He's a far cry from golden-haired Brian in his fleece-lined corduroy jacket. But Steve has something that stands out: charisma. Everyone adores him.

I think back to junior year of high school, when a popular boy in my class named Peter asked me out. He liked dating girls outside his clique. When he did, those girls—girls like me—rose instantly in social rank, jumping multiple rungs overnight.

The Monday after my first date with Peter, I was in the school library when one of his friends, Scott, walked in. We'd gone to school together for five years, and not once had Scott ever spoken to me. Not a hi or hello.

As I glanced up from my book, Scott looked me in the eyes and smiled. "Hi," he said simply.

"Hi," I replied.

So that was it. That's all it took to be acknowledged by the jock crowd—a stamp of approval from Peter.

Could it be the same now? Could dating Steve earn me a place among this crowd?

By this time, my weight gain has taken its toll. Feeling fat and un-attractive, I'm on the hunt for a pathway to positive attention that might quiet the self-loathing.

So, when I run into Steve on campus or at parties, I tilt my head, scrunch my nose, and laugh at his jokes as if I adore him too. It's not long before he asks me out, and we start dating.

A few weeks in, he and his crew plan a spring-break weekend in Myrtle Beach, and I'm invited to enjoy a rental house one block from the beach, a Saturday pig picking with endless kegs of beer.

The drinking begins as soon as we arrive. Within hours, one of the girls stands on a coffee table, singing along to Tom Petty's "Don't Do Me Like That." I watch her bounce her head back and forth, fist at her mouth like a microphone. Her voice is raspy, as if she's swallowed sand or smoked too many Marlboros. She looks wholesome, a quintessential beach girl with wavy blond hair and freckled cheeks. Mostly, I notice what she's wearing: shorts and a bikini top.

Standard fare at a beach party. Except for me. I haven't worn a bikini since the age of fourteen, and I rarely wear shorts. Today, carrying 20 pounds more than when school started in the fall, I'm wearing a shapeless blue sundress with yellow flowers. It hides every bump or bulge—unless I sit down. Then I have to tug and adjust, covering my legs, smoothing my stomach. Watching her, I fantasize about my next diet, imagining a summer when I'll be thin enough to wear shorts, a bikini top, and stand on a table without fear of breaking it.

Throughout the day, partygoers traipse like busy ants up and down the stairs to the kegs on the driveway. Trash cans overflow with red Solo cups, and the kitchen floor is so sticky that I don't dare remove my flip-flops. By 2:00 a.m., Steve and I stumble to bed.

Within minutes, he rolls on top of me, his weight pressing all the air from my lungs. He stinks of Doritos, sweat, and Budweiser. We haven't had sex—not even kissed seriously. I'm completely uninterested in anything physical. I'm here for company, not intimacy. Or sex.

I want to push him away, but I don't. Saying no feels unacceptable. I tell myself that I owe him something—for the house, the beer, the ride, the attention. Can't expect something for nothing, can I?

I slam my eyes shut and turn my head, hoping to get it over with. My mind drifts above the bed, fuzzy and distant. Once he's done, he rolls over and passes out. I snap back, blinking into the inky night, my head buzzing with questions: Wasn't I once considered pretty? Too pretty for someone or something like this? Why didn't I say no? Did I really owe him something?

The thoughts add up to one desperate question: What the hell am I doing?

The next morning, the party starts early with the guys prepping the pig. But Steve won't speak to me. I recognize it immediately. The silent treatment. He's punishing me, though he's got no idea that his silent treatment has nothing on Mom's. I'm unfazed.

As the day progresses, I wonder if he's upset because we slept together. Have I fallen victim to the Madonna/whore complex—where a woman is either virtuous and marriage material or slutty and disposable? How is this still happening after the feminist movement and the sexual revolution? I thought women were supposed to be free to explore, to say yes without shame. Apparently not. Here in a trashed North Carolina beach-house rental, the double standard is thriving.

By late night, my head dull from too many beers, I'm ready for sleep. Steve follows. I climb into bed and immediately turn my back to him. I'm not brave enough to say what I really think and feel. My own silent treatment will have to suffice.

On Sunday morning, his mood shifts. Before leaving the bedroom, he corners me and whispers, "Last night, when you turned your back, I wondered if maybe you regretted what we did."

"I did," I admit.

"Good. I'm glad to hear that."

Apparently, I get a do-over. For the next several weeks, he treats me with great deference, convincing himself I might be more like the Madonna after all.

In mid-May, we travel with two friends to a swanky wedding at the Union League Club in Philadelphia. After a five-hour open bar, the guys can barely stand. Steve throws me the keys, telling me to drive back to the hotel.

With no map and no sense of where to go, I get lost within a few blocks. Turn after turn, I drive in circles. None of the guys are any help.

Then, Steve mumbles from the backseat, first under his breath, then louder: "Blow me, Kim. Just blow me."

At first, his friends laugh. After repeated insults, they grow quiet, though they don't come to my rescue. Jeff, who's sitting in the front seat, looks down at his hands and picks at his nails. I glare at Steve in the rearview mirror. His head bobs, as armpit stains spread across his blue dress shirt and the buttons strain over his belly. Finally, he shuts up, passing out against the window.

Good Lord, what am I doing with this guy? I'm disgusted—not just by him, but by my own actions. I brought this on. If I hadn't used him to try to enter the friend group, I wouldn't be in this mess. It's not about him; it's about me.

But how did I land here? What type of woman am I trying to be? Parts of me are compliant because I've been conditioned to avoid conflict. Other parts are fiercely independent and rebellious. More like Mom.

Which parts serve me best? It's unclear. I only know I don't want to be like Mom. Yet I also don't want to endure emotional abuse just to be liked or to have friends. I grip the steering wheel, staring straight ahead, looking for a gas station where I can get directions.

By the time we reach the hotel, I've decided I won't put up with being treated like this. I deserve so much more. Love. Kindness. Peace. The next morning, I break up with Steve and launch an earnest effort to get my shit together.

•••

Home for the summer, I swell with equal measures of pride and pity. I dumped Steve, finished my first year of college, and earned decent grades. But I'm also fat, untethered, and anxious about my drinking.

If alcoholism runs in the family and ruined Dad's life, how will I know if I'm drinking too much? Or if I'm an alcoholic?

I throw myself into books about alcoholism, discovering the work of Adult Children of Alcoholics. On their "Laundry List" of fourteen traits, I score high, despite not growing up in the same house as Dad. I read Trait No. 4 again and again: *We either become alcoholics, marry them, or find another compulsive personality to fulfill sick abandonment needs.*

That's not the life I want.

I devour more self-help books, reading *The Road Less Traveled* and *I'm OK — You're OK*, and falling asleep to Sally Jessy Raphael's late-night radio advice show. I absorb all the wisdom I can. If what the experts say is true, it's possible to create a life that differs from how I was raised—a life without anger, cruelty, and dysfunction. I can monitor and manage my own actions and behaviors. I can surround myself with goodness. I can be different from Mom. And I can be different from Dad.

They say alcoholics can't just have one drink. As a test, I decide to stop after one drink whenever I'm at a bar. If I succeed, maybe I don't have the alcoholism gene. Besides drinking, I also cut back drastically on eating, shedding a quick twenty-five pounds in three months. I'm not ready to sport a bikini or shorts, but I'm feeling better about myself.

When I begin my sophomore year, I'm relieved that Steve has apparently dropped out and isn't returning to school. That means I can still hang out with the larger crowd of friends. Because we'd spent so much time together, Jeff and I pal around. While quiet and nonconfrontational in Philadelphia, he's kind, funny, and makes me laugh.

Months pass. Our friendship deepens. One evening, on a walk back to our dorms through campus, he stops. "I feel like we're becoming more than friends."

"Yeah, me too," I reply.

"But I worry about Steve."

"Mm-hmm." I understand, though I don't care about Steve's feelings.

He steps closer, fingers lacing in mine, and kisses me softly under the lamp-lit path. We pull back, giggling—nervous but excited.

Our relationship unfolds slowly, built on friendship. It's safe, soft, and steady. I reclaim my dignity and self-respect, free from drunken regrets.

Chapter 13

Prior to spring break, I have a brainstorm. Now twenty, I feel grown-up and mostly on my own, wondering if the life I'm building includes Dad. There are so many unresolved issues between us. Can we have a relationship? Or will he always remain on the sidelines, in the shadows?

I decide to travel to Florida to see him, so we can have a real heart-to-heart talk. I want him to see that I'm okay. I'm not asking for anything from him. I'd like a relationship—and to have some answers. Chief among them: Why did he disappear?

I reach out to ask about a visit. He and Joyce agree. I book a round-trip ticket from Dulles to Orlando, where they live. I'll stay five days, arriving Sunday and returning Thursday—enough time to travel to and from school.

On the morning of the trip, my hands are sweaty, my mouth dry, my heart racing. It's been ten years since we've seen each other. Will I recognize him? Will he recognize me?

My flight lands in Orlando around 10 p.m. I walk down the jet bridge into the gate area, scanning the sea of faces for my dad where friends and family typically meet their arriving passengers. All around me, travelers reunite with laughter and tears. I weave through the crowd to an open area, trying to get my bearings. I don't see him anywhere.

Though I've flown solo plenty of times before, I've never arrived some-where without someone waiting for me. Being in an unfamiliar airport is unsettling. I can't believe he's not here.

I sit down and dig through my purse for change to call Jeff. It'll be a long-distance call, so I need several coins. I find dollar bills, a few dimes, some pennies, and wadded-up Big Red gum wrappers. I pull out a Virginia Slim, light it with my yellow Bic, and take a long drag while I consider my options. Nervous excitement turns to fear and disbelief.

If I'm stranded in Orlando, what am I supposed to do? Fly to Pittsburgh to see Jeff and his family? Go home?

I shake the thoughts from my head. First things first: Head to baggage claim, and get change for the phone. Scanning for signs for baggage claim, I hear an announcement over the PA system: "Kim Vajta, please meet your party at Terminal B, Baggage Claim Area 5."

Terminal B? Where is that? I don't even know where I'm standing. But at least he's here. I just need to find him.

I follow signs frantically, realizing I must take a people mover from the gate to the terminal. The airport is massive. Several minutes pass until I determine which train to board. By the time I arrive in Terminal B, it's been fifteen minutes since my name was paged. Then another five minutes before I find the right carousel.

It's 11:30 p.m. now. The place is deserted except for my lone suitcase sitting off to the side. Dad is still nowhere in sight.

I trudge over to the customer service desk, deflated. The woman gives me five dollars in change so I can make some calls. The quarters rattle heavily in my purse.

Pulling the handset from the payphone and digging for Dad's number, anger rises. How could he just leave? Wouldn't he be worried if I didn't show up? Shouldn't he have checked whether I'd landed?

I dial. It rings several times before the answering machine picks up. "Dad," I say, trying not to cry or yell. "I'm here at the airport. I heard my name over the PA but had trouble finding the terminal. Can you come back for me?"

I call every five minutes. Each time the machine answers, I want to slam down the phone—but I don't. I also don't leave any more messages.

After midnight, Joyce finally answers. We've never spoken, and I'd rather this not be our first conversation.

"Where are you?" she asks.

"Joyce, may I speak to my dad, please?"

She passes him the phone.

"Dad, I'm at the airport," I say, masking my anger. I can't start this long-awaited visit with an argument. "I heard my name over the PA but couldn't find my way. Can you please come back?"

"Oh sure, hon," he says. "But it'll take about forty minutes to get there."

I tell him where I'll be, hang up, and sink into a cluster of bright-orange couches.

Fifty minutes later, he's beside me. I stand, relief flooding my chest. We hug and I swallow hard, trying not to cry—but the emotion wins.

"I'm sorry," I say. "I'm just excited to see you."

He hugs me again. "Kim, this is Joyce," he says, turning toward her.

"Hi," I say, extending my hand before leaning in for a hug—it feels more personal than a handshake.

She's nothing like I expected. Pale and lumpy, with hair set like my grandma's generation. She looks older than I imagined. They both do. I don't know how old she is, but Dad's only forty-two.

Nerves return. I'd prepared for weeks—what I'd say to Dad, how he'd respond—but I never once considered how I'd interact with Joyce. In the mental script I'd rehearsed, she didn't even have a role.

Still, I know how to win people over. I pepper them with questions, focusing my charm on her. But she's stiff and guarded, offering only short answers.

When we reach their townhouse, it's late. They show me to the lower level—a small rec room with a pullout sofa, an end table with a phone, a wall of bookshelves, and a tiny black-and-white TV. I say goodnight as they head upstairs. Exhausted and wired, I light a cigarette, flicking ashes into the toilet before crawling into bed and falling asleep.

By the time I wake and come upstairs, it's midmorning. Dad's already left for work. Joyce says he'll be home at 5:30. She doesn't work and hasn't made any plans for the day—or for me.

So I decide to take advantage of the Florida sun. I spend the afternoon in my bathing suit on the sidewalk, reading magazines and smoking cigarettes. The concrete is hard and hot, but better than being inside with Joyce. I've already concluded we won't be friends.

When Dad returns that evening, he says he's taking the next two days off so that we can go to Disney World, SeaWorld, Cape Canaveral, and Daytona. I'm thrilled and relieved. At least we'll get some time together. He also asks me not to smoke in the house.

Over the next two days, we embark on whirlwind adventures. But like a clingy toddler, Joyce never leaves his side. She sits next to him on the tour bus while I sit behind them. She refuses to let him ride rollercoasters with me.

"I don't want him to have a heart attack and die," she says. So I ride alone, thinking about how unfun Disney World is.

She doesn't give us a moment alone. I start to believe it's deliberate. How can she not recognize the importance of this reunion? Wouldn't she want the same for her own daughters?

I'm disappointed that Dad doesn't push for alone time either. Mostly, though, I blame her. I decide she's painfully insecure and that I don't like her one bit.

For petty revenge, when they go to bed at 9 p.m.—unthinkably early—I sneak downstairs and call Jeff and anyone else I can think of, running up their long-distance bill. It's the least he owes me.

By Thursday, I'm eager to leave. The heart-to-heart I'd imagined never happens. My hopeful reunion was just a one-sided fantasy. Dad is everything I've tried to deny he is—cowardly, selfish, unreliable, small. And yet I still love him.

I remember the dad who sat me on his lap to read, who tossed me high across the pool, who smiled with that gold-toothed grin and twinkling hazel eyes. It's not just the *idea* of a dad that I miss; I miss the dad I remember. The one I thought I knew but didn't. And now, spending time with him in person, it's obvious he's still drinking.

Bewildered and disappointed, I hug him goodbye at the airport. After nearly a week together, we are no closer than we were last week—when we hadn't seen or spoken to each other for years.

Chapter 14

Over the two years that Jeff and I date, I visit his family in Pittsburgh during holidays and summer break. His parents, married for more than two decades, remind me of *Leave It to Beaver*. Their home is calm, loving, and structured: prayers before meals, Sunday mass, laughter, and kindness. They are gentle with one another. No raised voices or furrowed brows.

I watch, awed and slightly embarrassed. Adult kids baking cookies with their parents? That seems like fictional TV at its best. I've been fooled before into thinking what I'm witnessing is real life. Yet they seem genuine. Seeing their marriage and home life sparks questions for me about what leads to harmony and lasting commitment.

Even though I know Jeff and I aren't headed toward marriage, I wish I could unlock his parents' secrets and hold them for the future, for whenever I find my forever partner.

• • •

There's a common storyline about mothers and daughters: They clash when the daughter is a teen, then grow close as she matures. That's been my hope.

I'm proud of Mom in many ways—partly because she's so unlike other moms: a single mother, a Mexican woman, carving a path in a male-dominated field, with no one to rely on or share parenting duties. Maybe she had no choice but to be strict, to control my every move. Maybe that's what a single mom with a demanding career requires.

I've been out of college for nearly a year now, living back home. Little, if anything, has changed between us, despite the letter she sent freshman year. I thought by now we'd be different—that we'd find common ground, that she'd respect the fact that I'm responsible, launching my advertising career, making good decisions. Somehow, I thought her anger at me would have subsided.

But we are not that mother-daughter story. If I hadn't witnessed my friends' evolving relationships with their moms, I'd think that whole idea was bullshit, a myth.

When she's angry, I stay out of her way. But because she and her boyfriend, Russ, argue constantly, even when I disengage from her, tension lingers in the air like smoke from a smoldering fire.

On this Mother's Day, 1985, Mom and Russ have gone away for the weekend. And all I can think is, *Who does that?* Who doesn't spend Mother's Day with their children? Is our relationship so meaningless that we can't even celebrate the one holiday meant for mothers and their children?

I spend the day sulking, watching TV, eating three-quarters of a bag of mini Nestlé Crunch bars from the freezer. I toss the wadded wrappers into the trash and go back to the couch.

A few hours later, they return. I'm still in the same spot.

"Hey," I grunt.

"What are you doing?"

"Not much. Watching a movie."

"What is this?" Her voice rises. She's staring into the trash can.

"What?"

"All these candy wrappers! You ate all this? No wonder you're so fat, if this is what you do all day—watch TV and eat candy!"

"Stop. I had some chocolate. What's the big deal?"

"You're kidding yourself, young lady, if you think you can—"

"Oh my gosh, stop. Get off my back."

"Don't tell me to get off your back. I'll do and say whatever the hell I want. This is my house!"

"Fine. Sorry," I say sarcastically, turning off the TV and heading to my room.

Heart thumping, I want to throw something or cry or both. I'm twenty-two, making $12,000 a year, still living at home—and something in me snaps. I'm tired of her volatility. I can't live like this anymore. I need to be free from her.

I call friends, desperate for a solution. One says she knows someone looking for a roommate while her fiancé is away with the Air National Guard. We meet the next day to look at apartments in Alexandria. By Thursday, we sign a lease.

Friday night, I tell Mom while she's making dinner.

"I'm going to be moving out," I say, steadying my voice.

"Oh, you are, are you?"

"Yes. I found an apartment in Alexandria. I'll share it with a friend of Ann's."

She shakes water from lettuce leaves into the sink. "Well, good for you."

"I'll be moving tomorrow. Is it okay if I take my bedroom furniture?"

"Yes, that's fine. There are a few other things in the basement you might want."

She turns back to her salad, lost in thought. With her, I never know what to expect, though I'm always braced for the worst. But she doesn't seem angry or sad, which is a relief. Maybe she's relieved in her own way. Perhaps she's just as eager for me to go as I am to leave. Maybe there is a slight shift between us after all. If I'm an adult capable of being completely independent, how does she have the right to begrudge me these types of decisions?

Saturday, I pack everything into my cream-colored Camry. A friend with a truck helps haul my bed and dresser, along with the gold tweed sofa and end tables Mom gives me.

The apartment isn't much—dark, overlooking the highway, doubling my commute—but it's mine. I can eat chocolate whenever I want. Without tension thickening the air, I unclench my jaw and drop my shoulders.

Over the next year, Mom and I see each other only occasionally. She never visits my place—though maybe I never invite her. I dog-sit when she travels, but otherwise, our lives rarely intersect.

Then she tells me she's moving back to California to take a new position at Lockheed, where her career began. She's negotiated a premium package that counts her early years there toward her pension. It's a great opportunity, another impressive step forward.

Despite the distance between us, I'm sad she's leaving. My romantic notion of what we *could* be still lingers. I don't give up easily. I'm also sad to be alone again with no family nearby and no safety net. In the past, if things got desperate, I could turn to her. Now, it'll be just me. That's terrifying.

I think back to being seven, out on a small fishing boat with Dad and a friend of his. At dawn, we were so far from shore, there was no land in sight. The ocean stretched endlessly in every direction. It was the first time I couldn't see land—and it was unnerving.

I looked over the side at the clear water and the layers of translucent jellyfish floating below, hundreds of them.

"I don't like this," I said, scooting closer to my dad. "I can't see any land."

"Everything's gonna be fine," he said.

A few minutes later, he frowned at the compass.

"Hey, Bob, how do you read this thing? Is this broken?"

"Gosh, Larry, I have no idea."

"How are we going to get back to the marina?" Dad asked.

"I dunno. Good question!" Bob said, shrugging.

My stomach dropped. Were we lost? How would we get back? Blood pulsed in my ears.

"Dad! Are we lost?" I squealed, imagining falling into a vat of jellyfish.

They looked at me, then burst out laughing. The compass was fine. It was a joke, they said. I never understood how or why Dad thought it was funny to play such a cruel joke on me when I was so young. But I've never been in a position of feeling safe and confident in his love or availability to question or challenge what he did.

Now, here I am, truly on my own—paying bills, managing my life— with those same old fears stirring. The terror feels familiar, echoing that childhood moment, scanning the horizon for land.

If Mom's no longer on the East Coast, who will I turn to if I'm in trouble? Who can I trust to read the compass?

PART TWO

Chapter 15

I'm twenty-four years old on St. Paddy's Day weekend, 1987, when a big group of friends and I roll into the fourth-annual Rally in the Alley party. It's held in the narrow passageways between 18th, 19th, L, and M streets NW, near two popular Irish bars in DC. Normally, it's a dark crevice in the city where rats scurry and dumpsters spill over with beer bottles and trash bags. But today, kegs and bands take their place. We stand shoulder to shoulder, dressed in green, drinking from noon until dusk, long ago having abandoned my one-drink-only rule.

When the bash ends, my friends Sarah, Kyle, and I head to our friend Ben's house for an after-party. That's our usual weekend rhythm. We're regulars at the Black Rooster, Mr. Days, and the Bottom Line—where we know all the bartenders and most of the faces. If we don't, someone in our crowd does. It feels less like living in the nation's capital and more like belonging to a small, three-bar town.

At Ben's, I spot a handful of people around the table—and one familiar face. A guy I met about a year earlier, when a mutual friend, Beth, introduced us at the Bottom Line. That first meeting had not gone well.

Apparently, Beth had told him I was interested in meeting him, though I'd said no such thing. I hadn't even wanted to go out that night. I was in a mood and would've preferred to stay home, but Sarah convinced me. "It'll be good for you," she'd said. So I sat in a round booth, nursing a Toasted Almond and a bad attitude, when Beth appeared with a man in tow.

"I want you to meet my friend Harry," she said, then vanished into the crowd.

He slid into the booth next to me. "How's it going?"

"Fine."

"Where are you from?"

"McLean."

"Oh really. Me too."

He kept trying—peppering me with questions, looking for a spark—but I wasn't having it. My answers were short, clipped, and meant to send him on his way. When was this guy going to get the hint?

After a few minutes of silence, he said, "Ya know what?"

"What?"

"You are wound *waaaay* too tight," he said. "You really need to loosen up." Then he stood, grabbed his drink, and walked away.

I wanted to tell him to fuck off. He didn't know me. I could be fun. And loose.

Months later, I saw him again at a Halloween party. He was dressed as a paper bag with a hole for his face and the words HAVE YOU SEEN THIS CHILD? written across the front—a parody of the missing kids campaign. It made me laugh. We didn't talk, but of all the costumes that night, his was the one I remembered.

And now, here he was again, across the table at Ben's. I probably deserved to be told off that night, but it was bold of him to say it, especially since Beth was our mutual friend. I grab a beer, take a seat, and hope we can both pretend that night never happened.

Hours pass. We drink, laugh, tell stories. Zeppelin blares through Ben's Bose speakers. Eventually, Harry and I find ourselves talking one-on-one.

"So, what do you do?" I ask.

"I own a private investigations business. McLean Investigations."

"Oh, that's cool."

"How about you?"

"I'm in advertising."

That's the start of a conversation that lasts for hours. He wants to know about advertising—how to attract clients, whether Yellow Pages ads work, what catches the eye. We pull the thick directory from a table under Ben's landline and flip through ads for investigative firms, comparing layouts and slogans, critiquing his competition.

It's a simple, easy exchange, but somewhere in the middle of it, I realize I like him. He's funny and kind. Nothing like the guy I'd written off a year earlier. And since we're getting along, I have no reason to bring up our first meeting—or the version of me he met that night.

Over the next few weekends, we see each other often, always in the same small circle of friends. He's two years older, a Catholic-school grad from across town. His best friend is Beth's older brother, so it seems inevitable that our paths had crossed before.

We're not dating, exactly. Just circling each other. What I don't realize yet is that our friend Jimmy is playing Cupid, encouraging Harry to ask me out. "She likes you, man," he tells him. Harry's not convinced, having fallen for that trick a year earlier when Beth introduced us.

Then, four weeks after Rally in the Alley, a card arrives at my office. It's an oversize Hallmark card showing the Easter Bunny tossing colorful eggs, and inside it reads: DON'T EAT THOSE BROWN-COLORED EGGS! I laugh out loud and tack it to my bulletin board. When I call to thank him, he asks me out for Saturday, the night before Easter.

• • •

Our first official date is at McKeever's, a local Irish pub in McLean. He picks me up at the condo Mom owns—one of her investment properties before she moved back to California. Sarah and I rent it from her, splitting the mortgage and taking care of the place.

The date lasts all night and rolls into the next morning, when we decide to stop for Easter brunch at the Holiday Inn—two twenty-somethings in stale clothes without a reservation on a high holy day. The hostess tells us the wait is forty-five minutes. We look at each other and shrug.

"Sure, that's fine," we say, settling onto the lobby bench. Pastel-clad families stream by, a contrast to my wrinkled clothes smelling of cigarettes and beer from the night before. It's obvious we skipped Easter Mass. But none of that matters. The world falls away. All we care about is talking, laughing, and staying in each other's company.

That Easter brunch line turns out to be the longest wait we'll ever share. In time, I'll learn that Harry has no patience for waiting. If he sees a line, he wants a Plan B—another restaurant, another time, another day. But that morning, he was on his best behavior, and I like to think he found the wait worth it.

• • •

I fall hard and fast. When we're apart, I ache for him. He takes up every inch of space in my brain. More than anything, he makes me laugh. I've never been quick or witty—my funny thoughts arrive late, when the moment's already gone. But I'm an excellent audience for those who are. I get the jokes. And around Harry, I laugh all the time. It feels good. It feels new.

Harry and I become inseparable. Every weekend brings a new adventure: road trips, canoeing the Shenandoah with his dog, Mac, camping at Jellystone in a leaking tent, cheering ponies at the racetrack, rafting the Youghiogheny River in Pennsylvania. We sing along to homemade mixtapes in his white Ford hatchback: Fine Young Cannibals, 10,000 Maniacs, Talking Heads, John Mellencamp, Stevie Ray Vaughan. Sometimes we plan ahead, booking a Victorian inn in New Hope, Pennsylvania. Other times, we just drive until we find a place. I feel so grown-up—working by day, exploring the world with him by night.

By the time my twenty-fifth birthday rolls around that November, I know I want to spend my life with him. That doesn't necessarily mean marriage, just that I can't imagine life without him.

At the time, I'm smoking nearly two packs of Virginia Slims a day. I smoke everywhere—restaurants, the office, my car. At work, I light one cigarette from the last, lipstick-stained butts resting on the rim of my gold glass ashtray.

One day, I realize: If I ever lost even one day with Harry because of smoking, I'd never forgive myself. So, on my birthday, I quit cold turkey. I'm more hooked on him than on nicotine. Nothing has as tight a hold on me as he does.

Still, I fear he'll leave. Everyone I've ever loved—or who should have loved me—has left. The fear of abandonment runs deep, silent but constant. I don't think about it much during the day, but at night, it surfaces in vivid dreams.

The Harry in my nightmares isn't the man I know. Midnight Harry is cruel and faithless—he abandons me, betrays me, mocks me. He's a lying, cheating version conjured by my oldest fear.

Eventually, I start telling him about the dreams. When I wake and say, "You won't believe what I dreamed last night."

His deadpan reply is always the same: "What did I do now?"

The dreams never stop completely, but they soften over time—like the remnants of an old wound that's still healing.

Chapter 16

On Veterans Day, November 1987, I wake up, get ready for work, and head out for my commute from Annandale, Virginia, to Gaithersburg, Maryland, where I work at a small advertising agency. Normally, the drive around the Capital Beltway and up I-270 takes twenty-five or thirty minutes, but because it's a midweek holiday and most federal workers are off, I expect a smooth ride.

But forecasters are calling for early flurries.

I climb into my car just as large, sticky flakes begin to fall—softly at first, then steadily. The roads turn slick, and traffic slows to a crawl. By the time I reach the Cabin John Bridge—ten miles from home—we're inching forward through several inches of heavy slush.

An hour later, I pull into the office lot, trudge through the snow, and climb the stairs. I jiggle the front-door handle. Locked. No one's there. It hadn't even occurred to me to stay home. I'm so focused on doing well at work, proving myself, that skipping a day feels unthinkable.

With no way in, I tromp back to my car, frustrated by my own determination. Who drives an hour in a snowstorm just to find an empty office? Now I have to do the drive all over again—this time through even worse weather.

The return trip is brutal. After three hours of crawling through bumper-to-bumper traffic at five miles per hour, my car gives up. The engine dies mid-slush. I pound the steering wheel. "Damn it! Now what?"

I'm still five miles from home with no cellphone, no emergency kit, no blanket or food—nothing but my purse. I'm wearing slacks and pumps, hardly snow gear. I'm twenty-five, for heaven's sake. I don't plan for disasters. It's November! It never snows in DC in November.

I grab my purse, slam the car door, and start walking along the shoulder. I don't think to leave my flashers on or hang a white flag of surrender. I just abandon the Camry in the left lane and trudge into the swirling snow.

Each step is a slide. My hair clings wet to my head; my toes go numb. Cars creep past, drivers staring straight ahead, warm behind their fogged windows.

Then a Jeep slows beside me. The window rolls down, and a woman leans out. "Hey—where are you headed? Want a ride?"

"Oh, yes!" I croak. "I'm going to Annandale—Route 236."

"Perfect. I'm going to Springfield. I'll drop you at the exit."

I scramble in, flooded with relief and gratitude. When we reach my exit, she pulls to the shoulder and lets me out. I thank her profusely before setting off on foot again, a mile or so to go.

With each step, my self-pity deepens. I can't believe I had to abandon my car. What if it's damaged or stolen or gone forever? How will I get it back? And how much will this cost?

By the time I reach the condo, I'm soaked through. Sarah's on the couch when I burst in. Her eyes widen.

"Oh my God, what happened?" she asks, horrified, then pauses before howling with laughter.

"Don't laugh! It was awful," I whine, but she can't stop.

I strip off my wet clothes and stand under the shower, letting the hot water thaw me. I'm not just tired from the day; I'm weary from doing everything alone. Mom offers no guidance. Not even on things she prides herself on, like paying bills or fixing a light switch. She's three thousand miles away, both literally and emotionally. There's no one else to lean on, no mentor or older voice of reason. I've learned to muscle through life, figure it out myself, fail, regroup, and try again.

But maybe things are different now.

I call Harry once I'm warm and calm, explain the whole ordeal. We agree to go back for the car once the roads clear. Just making that plan loosens something in me. Maybe I don't have to do *everything* alone.

By nightfall, the snow has piled a foot deep. The next morning, Harry drives over but doesn't deliver the news I want. His route from his parents' house to mine is the same stretch of beltway where my car broke down.

"It's not there anymore," he says. "It must've been towed."

"Towed?" I nearly screech. "How do you even find a car in this city? There are millions of people, hundreds of tow companies!"

He promises we'll track it down, but first he needs to run errands for his mom. He'll be back that afternoon.

With the city buried and my car gone, there's nothing to do but wait. I curl up on the couch and turn on the soap operas I haven't watched in years. *All My Children, One Life to Live, General Hospital.* Comfort TV. Nostalgia. I'm nine again, watching with my stepmother, Carolyn, at the house in Long Beach after Kerry was born. Later, in college, I'd watched with my dorm floor every afternoon; thirty of us glued to the screen when Luke and Laura married in 1981.

By the time Harry returns, it's dark outside—and he's grinning. "Good news," he says. "I found your car."

He'd spent the afternoon calling every towing service clearing cars from the beltway, tracking it down while I sat watching daytime drama.

I throw my arms around him, tears spilling. "Thank you," I whisper.

It's not that I want a rescuer. I don't need someone to solve my problems. But his kindness stirs something deep in me—a long-dormant sense of safety. Maybe I don't have to white-knuckle my way through life anymore. Maybe someone *will* think about me, without being asked.

Maybe I can have someone to turn to for advice, for help, for comfort.

Maybe I'm not going to have to go through life alone after all, drifting in a boat with no land in sight and a broken compass.

Chapter 17

In December, I plan to fly back to California for the holidays. The night before my trip, Harry and I go to dinner at our favorite Chinese restaurant. Perched at the bar, he begins peppering me with questions about my hopes, my values, my vision for the future. They're the kind of questions that make me pause and turn inward—what matters most, what I want my life to stand for.

It's not the first time we've ventured into deep territory. We often talk about our childhoods, our views on faith and spirituality, our philosophies, dreams, and fears. It's one of the things I cherish most about us. Our conversations meander like a long, colorful skein of cashmere yarn: soft, continuous, impossible to know where one thread ends and the next begins. I share as openly with him as I do with my girlfriends, maybe more.

But tonight feels different. There's an undercurrent, an unspoken weight. I sense we're both taking stock—not just of each other, but of what's ahead as well. I seize the moment to turn the tables, sprinkling my own questions into the mix. It becomes an interview in both directions.

I've spent an inordinate amount of time imagining the life I want and even more clarifying what I don't. I long for a family that feels whole and loving, the kind I never had growing up. Though I was raised to believe women could and should "have it all," I also yearn for something deeply traditional. The endless afternoons I spent watching *Leave It to Beaver* and

The Brady Bunch left their mark. Yet I also want to be *That Girl* and Mary Tyler Moore—independent, stylish, ambitious.

I want it all, a vibrant career *and* a warm home filled with laughter. I won't have latchkey kids waiting alone for me the way I once waited for my mom. I don't know how I'll pull off such opposing desires. But somehow I'm certain I will.

Because of the nature of our talks, I'm not afraid to share this vision. Swiveling on my barstool, sipping an Amstel Light, I lay it all out. He listens intently, then tells me his own.

That night, I learn he wants to care for his mother someday, even moving her in if she ever becomes sick or is dying. His father passed away two years before we met, a quiet absence that lingers behind his steady composure. He tells me he wants two, maybe four children, depending. He wants his wife home with them, though he says he supports a woman who works. Like me, he hasn't thought through how both can coexist, only that both matter.

Our childhoods couldn't have been more different. He grew up in a traditional Catholic home. His father headed off to work each morning, while his mother cared for their three children. Faith and family were the twin pillars of their lives. His parents were closer in age to my grandparents than to my mother.

And yet, beneath those differences, our values align almost perfectly.

When the evening ends and I fly west the next day, I know we've reached a turning point. We're either going to get married or we're not. While I'd be content to stay in this easy rhythm indefinitely, I know he wouldn't. That's not who he is. I can feel it: the quiet forward motion of something inevitable. Part of me wonders if there might be a ring waiting under the Christmas tree.

When I return from California, we exchange gifts, but no small velvet box appears. Still, Valentine's Day is around the corner, and we're still solid. My hope flickers on, steady as a pilot light.

For New Year's Eve, I plan dinner at my condo before we head to a party. I'm not, then or now, a particularly gifted cook, but I'm determined to make something special: Cornish game hens with snow peas in Dijon mustard sauce. I fuss in the kitchen all afternoon, plating each bird with care.

When the moment arrives, we carry our plates to the oversize mint-green velour sofa—a relic from my roommate's childhood home. The first bite sets our mouths on fire. Eyes watering, noses burning, we both start coughing and laughing at once.

I rush to the counter and grab the recipe. "One *tablespoon* Dijon mustard," it reads. My stomach drops. I used one *cup.*

"Oh my God, I totally screwed up," I say, panicking. "Here, let's wipe off the sauce."

We blot the poor birds dry with paper towels, then proceed to choke down what's left, laughing until we can barely breathe.

Laughter was a rare sound in my childhood home, but here it feels essential—the salt that seasons everything. You can live without it, but why would you want to?

When we finish, we set our plates on the coffee table. He bends down, reaching beneath the couch. I look at him, puzzled. Then he rises with a small box in his hand, drops to one knee, and opens it.

For a heartbeat, I can't process what's happening.

Did he just ask me to spend the rest of my life with him? After nearly killing him with a lethal dose of Dijon?

Oh my God. This is it. He's proposing.

Chapter 18

Our marriage begins beneath a blanket of blue skies on an unseasonably warm November afternoon. In the months leading up to the wedding, Mom's in a quandary. Should she bring Russ or her new boyfriend, Dell, as her date?

I don't have a strong opinion. Although she and Russ are no longer together, he's been a steady presence in our lives for more than a decade. But there's something different about Dell entering the picture. Mom's giddy when she talks about him, soft and giggly with a lilt in her voice. I've never seen her like this.

One day, she decides. Dell will be her escort. Russ will come as an invited guest.

My own quandary is who to ask to walk me down the aisle. Asking Dad isn't an option; I am not inviting that brand of chaos. What would I do if he simply didn't show up? It's entirely possible. Maybe even likely. I'm also not interested in asking Mom because my vision for the day feels more traditional.

For my entire life, I've been the daughter of a single, divorced mother and an absent father. It's the only family structure I know; It's my normal. Moments like these highlight the fact that my family makeup never resembles the cultural ideal. It makes me want to slink away in embarrassment, or to scream: "I'm sorry I'm different!"

I settle on asking Grandpa. We are not close necessarily; I grew up hundreds of miles away from where he lived, and he and Mom have a contentious relationship. Yet I know he loves me. Given I'm his first grandchild, he'll be honored just to be asked. Choosing him also means there'll be a sense of the traditional at our ceremony: the male patriarch giving the young bride away.

I think back to when I first introduced Grandpa to Harry, only a year and a half earlier, when I boldly invited him to California for my grandparents' fiftieth wedding anniversary. We'd been dating only two months, and even I didn't understand why I felt compelled to have him meet my entire family all at once. On paper, it made no sense. It was too much, too soon. I remember wanting to say to them, "Look at this great guy I'm dating. This decent, responsible, cute, funny person." I wanted to prove that despite Mom's relationship history, I wasn't a lost cause. I wasn't following in her footsteps.

At the celebration, Grandma shimmered in full-length gold, her charm bracelets jingling as she floated regally through the church. A spritz of floral perfume bloomed behind her. She hugged my mom, my aunts and uncles, and then each of us, her six granddaughters.

"Ahh, *mija*," she said to each one, the endearment that had evolved as we outgrew *mijita*, or my little daughter. Like a songbird, her voice trilled. It's not so much that she lit up the room; it was that we glowed in her presence.

Grandpa, dapper and proud, hugged us one by one and tickled our cheeks as he buried his walrus mustache in the napes of our necks. He surveyed the large family they'd built from next-to-nothing beginnings, cracked a joke in Spanglish, and nudged her with his elbow.

"Oh, *pues, papi*," she said as she blushed.

Grandpa was warm with Harry as well. Harry had braced himself for a reserved greeting or a protective interrogation. He'd expected something like, "Are you good enough for my granddaughter?" Instead, Grandpa welcomed him with charm and kindness.

Grandpa is delighted that Harry and I are planning to marry and says he would be honored to walk me down the aisle.

I also ask my sister, Kerry, now fifteen, to be a bridesmaid, and I invite Carolyn and her husband, Al. A few years earlier, I'd flown to Southern

California to reconnect with them, just as I'd tried to do with Dad. I confided in Carolyn about my Florida trip and shared my thoughts and disappointments. She'd grown bitter over his complete disregard for Kerry. There were no alimony payments and no attempts at parenting or building a relationship. He'd treated me poorly, but Kerry didn't even know him. He hadn't seen her since she was a baby. As we railed against his failures after years apart, Carolyn and I strengthened our bond.

Now, as Harry and I stand at the altar, long-held fears begin to slip away. I will not be alone after all. There's a chance to build the family I once imagined as I sat beside Rascal on the brown Naugahyde couch watching TV.

After we seal our vows with a kiss, I turn to see Mom in the front pew. Another fear softens. She's not outside in the pouring rain, watching from a window like Stella Dallas. She's here. And Carolyn is here too. It's a moment I could never have envisioned all those years ago, when Carolyn and I watched the movie and sobbed ourselves dry.

Chapter 19

For months after we take our vows, my feet barely touch the ground. I float—light, buoyant, unmoored—as if happiness itself has weightlessness.

I've never been this happy.

Whenever we're apart, it feels like a race to return to each other, as though there's a cost to missing even a moment of togetherness—to missing a single dose of the love, laughter, and safety that fills our shared orbit. When I'm out with friends, even those I adore, I find myself glancing at my watch until it's a respectable time to head home. Purse in hand, I hug my friends goodbye and rush back to him, to us, to the cocoon of our new life together.

I don't want to be the woman who loses herself in marriage, whose edges blur once the ring slides onto her finger. And yet here I am, wholly enveloped in the "we" we're becoming. It's everything I've longed for since childhood.

I throw myself into being a wife, as if I've stepped straight out of the glossy television families I once admired—never mind that they were scripted, make-believe. I dive into cooking, cleaning, and caring for my husband with a kind of eager devotion. It's as though I'm running toward the hooks where the garments of traditional gender roles hang, snatching the wifely suit with both hands and throwing it over my head without checking the size. Too small? Too large? I'll make it fit.

The truth is, cooking doesn't thrill me. Baking feels like a caloric trap. Laundry is pure drudgery, and the toilet and tub—best left unnamed. No matter how many times I cinch the domestic role tightly around me, it hangs awkwardly, oversize and dragging.

Maybe it doesn't fit anyone. Maybe we're all stumbling around in suits never meant for real bodies or real lives. But no one talks about it—and the chores still have to get done.

Among my friends, few are married. And of those who are—despite our coming of age in the shadow of second-wave feminism—traditional roles have quietly taken hold. Harry and I don't discuss it either. We don't consciously decide who does what. Our assignments are born of habit, history, and the quiet pull of my own longing for a stable, loving home. I take on the tasks because I believe they're the path to something better, richer, and more secure.

But being a homemaker isn't all I want.

I also want a career. I can't imagine not working, not striving toward something beyond the walls of our home. My mother wasn't exactly a bra-burner, but her message was clear: *Pursue a career. Be independent. Find work that matters.* It's so deeply ingrained, it feels cellular, with no resistance, no question. That's what she did. That's what I'm doing.

With one critical exception: for her, work was everything. More than me. More than relationships. Nothing outranked her ambitions.

I want my career to matter, but I want my family to matter more. My ambition is not for status or achievement. It's for connection. There will never be anything more important to me than that.

• • •

It's not until nearly a year into marriage that we have our first fight. The force of my anger shocks me. It rises suddenly, a geyser breaking through the calm surface of my chest. My mind floods with thoughts I can't organize quickly enough to speak. The more I try to make my point, the more the pressure builds.

Before I realize what's happening, I'm reacting, watching my hand grab one of the hurricane glass globes from the dining room table, a wedding gift from Carolyn, and hurl it against the wall. It shatters on impact, glass raining down across the plush white carpet.

Harry stands motionless, his expression unfamiliar. Then he turns and walks downstairs.

Instantly, panic replaces rage. I stare at the dent in the wall, the glittering shards at my feet. This isn't who I want to be. And I know it's not who he married. He won't tolerate this, at least not for long. I wouldn't either.

I scare myself with how quickly I lost control. The stakes crystallize in that moment: If I don't get a handle on this, I could lose everything.

A few days later, I pull out my old copy of *I'm OK — You're OK* and flip through the pages. I practice its advice in small, daily ways. I devour articles about relationships and communication. I tape *The Oprah Winfrey Show* to watch at night, taking notes whenever a relationship expert appears.

Harry and I sit down and agree to a few simple rules for arguing: no name-calling, no fuck-yous, no go-to-hells. We keep our pact. Arguments are rare, but when they do arise, I still struggle. I default to silence. The same weapon my mother used. Only mine isn't meant to punish; it's a shield against fear. I go quiet not because I want to hurt him, but because I'm afraid he'll leave.

It's a hard habit to break.

Chapter 20

A few weeks shy of our fourth anniversary, Harry stands to my right, a nurse to my left. They prop me up in the bed so that I can lean forward. My face nearly touches my knees. There's a thick smell of iodine and hospital sheets. I silently pray that I haven't shit myself.

I push hard.

Earlier, the doctor had reached inside to turn the baby, who was positioned "sunny side up." He might be easier to deliver face-down, he explained.

"One more push," the nurse says.

"Good job, honey," Harry adds.

"*Puuuush.*"

And then, there he is. A forehead. A nose. He's rotated back around to face me. The doctor catches the baby just as he slips free.

"It's a boy!"

Harry and I repeat it to each other, giddy, disbelieving: *a boy!*

I fall back, exhausted and proud, feeling like a total badass. I've never felt so strong.

I grew and delivered a baby.

• • •

Three days later, I am sitting on a pillow in a rocking chair in our bedroom cradling Justin when Mom walks in. I gaze up and smile. She's been a big help, arriving the same day we came home from the hospital, with plans to stay the week. Each day, she shuttles between the washer and dryer, washing onesies and spit-up rags, nursing bras and blankies. She stocks the freezer with meals made from scratch, buys groceries, and cooks dinner. Our new home, which we moved into only three weeks before, smells of fabric softener and sautéed onions.

I'm grateful for her support, yet something inside yearns for more. Can our shared experience of motherhood unlock a closeness that's never existed between us?

Plenty of friends talk about growing closer to their moms after having children. Why not us? Maybe this will be a turning point where we connect—really connect.

Mom watches me watching Justin.

"I had a hard time after you were born," she says. "Everybody said, 'Oh, you'll love the baby.' But I didn't feel it. I didn't feel that maternal bond."

I turn toward Justin to hide my face and my confusion. This isn't the opening to an emotional connection I hoped for.

Why is she telling me this? Does she think this is helpful? Is she trying to make this moment about her?

Regardless, it's not a conversation I want to have, even if her confession makes perfect sense. I've sensed it all my life. But I'm a new mom, for god's sake. One who's exhausted, sore, and sticky, and who just wants to be comforted and encouraged. To have my insecurities soothed. To be reassured that I'm going to be a good mom, that being a good parent is within reach.

For the next several minutes, I stare intently at Justin, turning her words in my head. What would it be like to not feel bonded to this little bundle?

She breaks the silence, "Do you need anything?"

"No, thanks. I'm good," I whisper, pulling Justin to my chest, nuzzling his neck, and smelling his downy soft hair.

• • •

When I was younger, I told friends I didn't want kids. My dreams weren't of having a husband and a family, even though I desperately wanted to be loved and cared for. I was going to focus on my career. And yet, I told myself, if I ever did have kids, I'd do it altogether differently than Mom. There would be no daycare, no babysitters. I'd never pawn off my kids on others, as she'd always done with me. I would be an ever-present fixture in their lives. They'd never wonder where I was or when I was coming back. Or whether they were loved. With me as their mom, they'd always feel at home.

Envisioning myself to be that kind of mom didn't mean I'd forsake my goals of having a career. Two years into our marriage, I started my own business, with motherhood in mind, figuring it would be easier to launch it before having kids than juggling new beginnings on both fronts at once.

Three days after we return from the hospital, the struggle to balance work and motherhood begins in earnest. As I nap beside Justin's bassinet, the house steeped in newborn stillness, the phone rings. A client's urgent request jolts me awake. As a freelancer, no work means no income. There's no maternity leave.

I sit up, turn on the baby monitor, press the cordless phone to my ear, and make my way downstairs. Lowering myself gingerly into the desk chair, still sore from the episiotomy, I power up the computer, finish the call with the client, and begin work on the project. I'm gripped by a quiet resolve to figure out how to straddle motherhood and career—as if I can give each my whole self, without letting one bleed into the other.

In that moment, I start spinning plates. Being ever-present for both work and children seems achievable, even though I've never watched anyone do it. Still, I'm convinced I can give a hundred percent to both.

I treat my business like a second child that is demanding, delicate, and deserving of just as much devotion. I wake early, working in the quiet before Justin stirs, then again during his naps. I set his bassinet beside my desk. I fold laundry with a phone clipped to my waistband and a headset looped around my neck. I take calls during feedings and diaper changes.

My biggest fear isn't exhaustion or inexperience; it's losing clients and opportunities—and money. I see myself not just as a mom, but also as a business owner and an entrepreneur. Failing to build a thriving business that can help to sustain us as a family would require the unthinkable: me getting a "real" job. And in my mind, that's not an option. That would mean relying on daycare and babysitters. I'd rather drive myself into the ground trying to realize my unwieldy dreams than fail at being the kind of parent I promised myself I'd be.

I will do all I can to make everyone—children and clients alike—believe they are my top priority. I don't realize yet how impossible my plan is.

But Justin is an easy baby. He sleeps through the night after two weeks, snoozes a full twelve hours no matter his bedtime, and dives for his crib at naptime. And when he's awake, he's a happy little guy. Plus, I'm not alone on this journey. I'm not a single mom. Harry also works from home, and we tag-team parenting duties.

• • •

Mom comes to town on occasion for business, always staying at the Ritz-Carlton nearby and stopping over for dinner. She's now married to Dell, and I like him. We're a lot alike. He's easy to talk to, gentle, kind, and nonconfrontational.

He too comes to town on business. One day, he suggests that Justin and I join him on an outing to Leesburg, to see the leaves and have lunch.

As we drive west on Route 66, the sky is a bold cerulean blue against a blur of bright umber and crimson trees. Justin—who's not quite a year old—sits cheerfully babbling from his car seat in the back.

Dell and I talk nonstop. He asks me questions about my childhood, about my dad, about my work. He's interested in all aspects of who I am and what I care about. I pepper him with questions too, in an easy exchange of information as we get to know each other better.

Once we arrive in Leesburg, we pull the stroller from the hatchback, strap in Justin, and walk up and down the town's sidewalks. The air is crisp and warm and smells of cider and honey. We peek into shop windows and read some of the plaques on the historic buildings. Justin drifts off to sleep for a morning nap as we wind our way through side streets and neighborhoods. At lunchtime, we decide to pop into a dimly lit tavern for a bite to eat.

As we sit laughing and talking quietly at a window table, he remarks on what a good boy Justin is and how he hasn't fussed or cried all day. I swell with pride, as if I had something to do with his sunny disposition.

When we finish our meal, I look around at the rest of the restaurant patrons. Technically, Dell is now my stepfather. Are any of these people father-daughter pairings? I've never really had a father-daughter outing. My long-ago visits with Dad and Carolyn were to amusement parks and zoos. This has been an intimate day laced with thoughtful conversation and deep connection, the type of day I longed to have with my own dad. It's what I fantasized about when I ventured to Florida.

As Dell pays the tab, I realize he's no longer just Mom's husband; he and I are developing our own relationship. Even after she and Russ had dated nearly ten years, he and I didn't have any type of meaningful relationship apart from theirs.

●●●

As Justin's first birthday nears, we've settled into an easy rhythm. I work in the early-morning hours, at naptimes, and in short spurts during the day. If I have meetings or important calls, Harry takes over, and vice versa. We take breaks to go to the park and eat lunch. I love the three of us having so much together time. I recognize what a luxury it is.

As often happens, the next few months bring about some major changes. Harry closes his business, lands a new job in a completely different field, and I discover I'm pregnant again.

Balancing two boys under two on my own and a growing client list is more challenging than I expected. Baby Jason isn't as cheery or as good of a sleeper as Justin was. What he wants most is to be with me, on me, held by me at all times. But I can't always comply. So once in a while, I let him cry it out in the bassinet by my desk while I hunch down on the bathroom floor to take a conference call, hoping the exhaust fan drowns out the noise beyond the door. It's an imperfect solution to an increasingly hard situation.

Still, I don't consider closing the business, getting a job, or stepping away from my career. I'm committed to making this work. Daycare and babysitters, reduced income, or no longer having a career are not options. So, I keep going—spinning the plates higher and faster.

Despite once upon a time thinking I may never have kids, I cling to a parenting philosophy that's percolated in my brain as far back as I can remember, well before I practiced parent-child conversations in the shower. A philosophy built on connection—the belief that to raise emotionally secure kids, I must be a consistent presence in their lives.

Present when they cry, fall, or reach for me. Available to cheer, comfort, or applaud. Present in the silence. In the rain. In the sunshine. There, always, for guidance, discipline, and to facilitate repair. Not pawning off my children on others, and never forcing them to contend with life all on their own. I'm determined to give them what I never had, even though I know I'm occasionally failing when it comes to execution. Will crying it out in a bassinet cause Jason irreparable harm?

I stumble daily trying to strike the right balance. Client calls interrupt. Deadlines loom. But still, I string together hundreds, then thousands, of small moments of togetherness. Cuddles. Storytime. Park outings. Playtime. Lullabies. Saturday-morning cartoons in our jammies on the couch.

I'm hopeful that my devotion—*our* devotion—to building a family will matter more than anything else I do in this lifetime.

• • •

When Jason is not yet a year old, I land a project that requires me to be on-site for a client meeting. Justin attends morning preschool now, but Jason has never been left with anyone besides family or trusted friends.

With Harry working out of the house, I'm forced to find a local daycare with drop-in services and book a slot.

That morning, I wrestle into a black pencil skirt and cream blouse. Both are too snug. My feet cram into heels; my bra straps dig into my shoulders. I'm already sweating by the time I buckle Jason into his car seat and toss the diaper bag under his feet.

On the drive over, I mentally calculate how long I'll be away. I picture him standing in a crib, crying and confused, waiting for me to come back. Will he feel abandoned like I often did?

The daycare is housed in an old elementary school. The infant room is painted robin's-egg blue and lined with cribs and cubbies. I feign a smile, keeping my voice cheerful and light. I don't want Jason to pick up on any hesitation.

I hand him over, kiss his cheek, and say brightly, "Be a good boy. I'll be back soon! I love you."

I walk briskly to the car, heels clicking against the pavement, trying to stay focused on the meeting ahead. I pull out of the parking lot and turn right to head toward the highway.

Half a mile out, my throat tightens. My stomach flips. And before I fully register what's happening, I'm gasping for air, vomiting onto my skirt.

My hands shake as I grip the steering wheel and swerve to the curb. I fumble for tissues from my briefcase, wiping sticky bile from my lap.

"What just happened?" I whisper.

In my desperate effort to parent differently—to rewrite the narrative I inherited—I've gone too far. I've bent myself into shapes no one asked of me. My body can't contain the emotional pressure I've created. I've puked all over myself.

And it's all self-imposed, driven by my near-rabid determination to give a hundred percent to parenting and to my clients. I've assumed this is what's required of me if I want to meet my goals of being a better mother than Mom was and cultivating a successful career.

This isn't healthy. Not for me. Not for my kids.

And yet, in this strange, humbling moment, one thing is clear: I am not my mother.

She didn't prioritize being a parent because it wasn't important to her. She admitted that she never felt the bond that makes someone willing to sacrifice for their child. That's not me.

I don't need to prove I'm different. I *am* different.

Somehow, when it comes to caring for the kids, I've conflated asking for help from others with parental neglect and disinterest. But they're not the same. There must be a middle ground, away from the extremes, where I can land.

Asking for help once in a while doesn't mean I'm a neglectful or an abusive parent. I can break the pattern without breaking myself.

Chapter 21

When Justin is not yet three years old, it's clear he's obsessed with sports—especially football. On Sundays, when Harry and his friends watch NFL games, Justin uses every commercial and halftime break to run to the basement, reenacting the plays he's just seen. Tucking a Pee Wee Football under his arm, he scores touchdown after touchdown.

At four years old and while attending summer camp, he's excited to play flag football, having practiced his moves in the basement for quite a while. He zigs and zags around the community center, zooming from one classmate to another, snatching scarves from their waist belts the moment the ball's in play. No one gets past Justin.

I've just arrived for pickup and am watching from the picture window—half amused, half embarrassed. He's much more competitive and in tune with the goal of the game than any of the other children. When camp ends, kids spill into the hallway where the other moms and I stand waiting.

"Did you see that boy?" a mom whispers to her friend. "He was assaulting the girls. Grabbing all the flags!"

I bristle at the word "assault" but don't say anything. Instead, I conclude that co-ed sports, classes, or camps—where the primary objective is "to have fun"—won't be a good fit for Justin. He wants to play hard. And win.

That same year, during his first soccer game when teams don't yet keep score, he walks off the field announcing exactly how many goals were scored by both teams.

"Oh, but we're not keeping score," the coaches say. There is no persuading him. He knows his team, the Yellow Stingers, won. By a lot.

At five and six, he has a full sports schedule, with Harry as a volunteer coach. School and sports provide structure for each season of our lives. Soccer in fall. Wrestling in winter. Lacrosse in spring. Practices are held three nights a week, with games, matches, or tournaments on weekends. And he can't wait to turn seven so that he can finally play youth football.

Like when the boys were babies, I want to be there for every moment, not simply dropping them off and heading elsewhere to do my own thing. There's nowhere else I'd rather be, nothing I want more than to watch from the sidelines. Not hovering or interfering. Just being there.

Early on, Jason plays beside me with other siblings on the sidelines. It's not long before we realize he's as competitive as Justin and eager to get in the games too. When he's old enough and because he's used to playing with older kids, he's allowed to "play up" on Justin's teams.

So in winter, I drag a book with me to wrestling practice but find myself watching Harry teach the young wrestlers new moves. I learn the difference between a hip heist and an ankle pick. Cheering from the stands on weekends, I yell, "Head up, head up. Hips! Hips!"

In spring, I watch the boys practice how to scoop, cradle, throw, and catch on the lacrosse fields. I pack coolers of healthy snacks and Gatorade, lugging smelly shoulder pads and sweaty gear in the back of my Chevy Suburban, keeping the windows down to air out the cab. I drive gaggles of boys to and from practices, listening intently to their conversations about Pokémon and the video game *Backyard Baseball.*

During dinners, as Harry and the boys recap that day's practice, game, or match, I hang on their every word, absorbing the nuances of what it means to be an athlete, and more importantly, what it takes to raise one. With Harry as the coach and technician, I become the emotional cheerleader.

The boys could have played or pursued anything, and I'd have immersed myself into every aspect of it. Not to micromanage or control their efforts, but to be there for them. I'm interested in what they're interested in. I want to hear and understand their thoughts. This is vastly different from Mom, who asks them only about what she's interested in: school, grades, books.

With both Harry and me actively involved in their lives, we're building a solid foundation of love, togetherness, and support for our young family. But we're also building a tight-knit community of fellow sports parents. And friends. I'm not the only one on the sidelines. Each night, moms and dads sit in collapsible chairs, side by side, week after week. With our boys often playing the same sports, our bonds grow with each successive season.

On Friday or Saturday nights, when practices or games end, families gather at the local dive bar. Boys crowd long tables, playing pinball and chasing one another around, while the parents laugh, eat, and drink until it's time to pack up and head home. I cherish these times, when we're all hanging out and cultivating friendships, marveling that I've found a place of deep comfort and great fun on the sidelines and in the gymnasiums of our small suburban oasis—me, the unathletic one who was always picked last for a schoolyard team.

When Justin turns seven, we say goodbye to the soccer fields in the fall and hello to football.

Chapter 22

While Mom and Dell typically stay at hotels when they're in town on business, they occasionally stay with us through the weekend. Once a year or so, we'll pack up the boys and head to California for a visit. Over time, I notice an odd pattern. When she's at our home, she is the perfect guest. Gracious and easy to be around. She'll jump in to help with laundry, cook batches of dinners for the freezer, and take the boys on outings to the city or the movies. I like this version of her.

Yet, when I'm on her home turf, she's decidedly different. All the old habits emerge. The *flap, flap, flap* of her slippers down the stairs each morning plunges me back to childhood and the ability to discern her mood. She might go hours or even days without speaking to me. By the end of the visit, I'm exhausted by the unending effort to assess and respond to the emotional temperature of every interaction, no matter how slight.

I also notice that I'm no longer the sole target of her wrath. Dell too is rocked by her whims of unpredictability. They bicker constantly. It frightens me to think that their marriage won't last and I might lose him in the fallout. How and why would a decent guy like him put up with this treatment?

After one particularly contentious visit, I decide to write her a letter expressing my thoughts. I don't mind hosting her at our home, but I'm no longer interested in visiting her in California because of the way she treats me.

"If you have something difficult to say, say it in a letter," she once counseled me. For once, I take her advice.

It doesn't go well. She doesn't call after receiving the letter. In fact, she stops speaking to me altogether.

Months pass, until one day my cousin Marisa calls.

"Did you hear the news?" she asks.

"No, what happened?"

"Grandpa died yesterday."

I lean back on my bed and stare at the ceiling, my heart dropping to my feet. I'm sad to hear the news, but even more so, stunned that Mom didn't call to tell me herself. She is harboring such resentment that she couldn't see beyond her anger enough to pick up the phone as a courtesy to tell me herself.

It shakes me to see the lengths she'll go to exact revenge. Who does that?

Worse, I know I can't attend Grandpa's funeral. Who knows what she might do if I show up? After years of sensing her moods and attempting to manage or lessen outbursts, her influence remains outsize. Without as much as an interaction with her, I can be bullied into submission. She still scares me that much. And I don't have the wherewithal to attend the funeral and battle her. While I love Grandpa, want to pay my respects, and see family, I'm too worn down. This time, she's won.

More months pass without the two of us speaking. What's noticeable is that I don't miss her. I rarely even think of her. But I do miss Dell. It begins to dawn on me that if I don't mend things with her somehow, I will lose Dell too. I make an internal calculation: Having her in my life is the only way I can maintain my relationship with him. It seems well worth the sacrifice.

I pick up the phone. When she doesn't answer, I leave a message on their voicemail, asking if we can find a time to meet and talk during her next business trip to DC.

We meet at a café at the local mall, between the Ritz-Carlton and my house. I've been fighting the urge to vomit all morning. I'm a forty-something-year-old woman with my own career and family who's terrified of her mother. Maybe, because we're in public, it won't escalate into ugliness.

Within minutes, our voices rise. Once more, I explain the points from my letter. I am desperate to make her understand. But she's having none of it. The argument devolves, and people are beginning to stare at us.

At one point, she turns to me stone-faced and says, "I think you're jealous of me."

I stifle a laugh. Is she serious? Does she not see all the ways I have built a life that bears no resemblance to hers? Does she not recognize the lengths I've gone to do life differently? To create a loving marriage. To be there for my kids. To put family above career.

She doesn't. She doesn't see any of it…or any of me.

I remind myself that this meeting isn't about us patching up our differences. This meeting is about getting on solid-enough ground so that I can resume a relationship with Dell. That's my goal.

Plus, trying to outmaneuver her is exhausting. So, rather than continuing the argument or attempting to change her mind any further, I pause and ask simply: "What can we do to move past this?"

I'm motivated to square things away so that I can see Dell again. I assume she must want to do the same so that she can see Justin and Jason. She adores the boys, and I've never said a disparaging word to them about her, preferring to let them have their own relationship with her and to come to their own conclusions over time. We apologize to each other and I hug her goodbye, grateful that I'll be able to talk to Dell soon. Were it not for him, it's likely we would've remained estranged forever.

Chapter 23

The hospital attendant slides the tray onto the rolling bedside table, jostling the plate, juice cup, and plastic utensils. A ribbon of steam curls through a hole in the plastic dome. He lifts the lid, revealing two limp slices of French toast garnished with a sprig of parsley and a wedge of orange.

It must be breakfast. Day Four of our hospital stay. The rhythm of real life outside these walls has gone silent. Here, days dissolve into nights. Only the arrival of meals hints at the time. I don't know what day of the week it is. I just know I want out.

Justin lies still in bed, groggy and gray. His hand rests in mine, soft and smooth, still a child's hand. But the darkening hair on his arms and faint shadow above his lip remind me that he's growing up—even though right now, he's slipping away.

He hasn't eaten much since we got here, too doped up to feel much of anything. They've diagnosed him with pancreatitis, from a football injury. But today, we're stuck watching him fade. His pain is sharper, more frequent. His cries pierce the antiseptic cheer of this bright, scuff-free room. It smells of fresh paint and disinfectants. I'm grateful for the privacy, for not needing to worry if his moans are keeping someone else awake.

Because Harry and I don't plan to leave Justin's side, our close friends Scott and Kris have swooped in, swiftly moving Jason to their house until we know what's going on. It's a comfort not to worry whether he's being well cared for.

That night, we pull out the bottom of the single club chair by Justin's bed so that it extends flat. We tuck a sheet into its sides and arrange our bodies strategically, trying to fit the two of us into a two-foot-wide, five-foot-long rectangle. We spoon our bodies together, my back compressed against his chest, his head in my hair, laying on our left sides, not sleeping.

On the second night, Harry and I try a different strategy, putting our heads at different ends of the chair and lying on our backs. We try to politely bury our feet into side crevices in the chair so that we're not kicking each other in the face. These are the lengths we are willing and able to go, contorting ourselves into infinite positions, to be sure we're there for Justin.

By the third night, we've given up sleeping, tossing and turning until daylight. All the while, we listen to the constant beeping of Justin's heart monitor and his intermittent moans, which seem to be growing increasingly urgent. I can tell the difference now between the moans he utters in his sleep and those that beckon us to his bedside.

A nurse walks into the room to take Justin's vital signs. She surveys the machines, reads the screen display, and glances down at the food tray.

"Justin," she says loudly so that he will stir from his stupor, "you need to eat your food if you want to get strong enough to go home."

He opens his eyes and looks at her, then over to me.

"Mom, I don't want to eat. It hurts too much," he says, his eyes pleading for me to make the pain go away, to make the nurse go away. I see weariness in his deep brown eyes.

"Well, you have to eat to get better," she scolds.

I reach over his bed to pick up the silverware from the tray. French toast is his favorite breakfast food. I slice off one piece, swirling it into sticky syrup.

I think back to all the breakfasts we've shared through the years, how Justin's chatter fills the spaces in between each bite and the many times I've reminded him not to talk with his mouth full. When he was a toddler and first learned to talk, I joked that he didn't realize that most people verbalize only a portion of the million thoughts that cross their minds. He, on the other hand, believed his newly developed language skills were ideal for sharing every single thought. *Mommy, did you see that yellow car? Do you know my favorite color is yellow? Hey, how come that man is standing there? I don't think my shoes feel good on my feet. These are my favorite socks, Mommy.*

Here, in this room, he is quiet in the moments he's not in pain.

I pick up the fork and urge him to eat. I want him to get better, so we can go home. I want him chattering at our kitchen table, talking with his mouth full, and wiping his chin on his sleeve.

We don't know yet that every bite triggers his pancreas to release corrosive enzymes into places they shouldn't go. We don't know we're feeding him poison.

He takes one bite.

Moments later, he curls in on himself, clutching his stomach and crying out. My body freezes. My instincts were wrong; his were right. Food won't heal him. Maybe the doctors won't either.

That afternoon, Harry and I sit side by side, knees touching, our fingers loosely intertwined. We say almost nothing. We've been sitting like this for days—trading crackers, pacing the hall, stealing glances at each other with wide, worried eyes. We're exhausted, frightened, hungry, and heartbroken. But we're in it together. Completely.

My phone chirps. It's Rich, a fellow football parent. A surgeon. He's heard about Justin's injury.

"Pancreatitis," I say. "He got kicked in the stomach during a tackle."

"Is he eating?"

"Tried French toast this morning. He took one bite. Then the pain kicked in."

Silence.

Then, measured and firm: "The pancreas is nothing to mess with. I'm going to call some colleagues. I'll call you back."

I don't ask what he means. I'm scared of the answer.

He calls back within minutes.

"Children's is willing to take him," he says. "Let's get him transferred."

I hand the phone to Harry. He'll ask the right questions, the ones I can't form.

• • •

Outside, the ambulance glistens in the sun. I clutch my phone, spinning it slowly in my hand. Justin's voice is soft.

"Mom?"

"I'm right here, sweetie."

The EMTs collapse the stretcher legs and slide him in. With each shift, he moans. I'm getting used to the sound, which terrifies me.

"I'll be in the front," I say. "Dad will meet us there. I love you."

A barely perceptible nod.

"I'm riding with you, buddy," the EMT says. He sounds young. Steady.

Sunlight presses down on my fleece. It's the first time I've felt the sun in days. I want to tilt my face toward it. Instead, I climb into the cab, legs dangling like a child's. I stare at my hands wrapped around my phone. I don't make small talk.

I should call Mom, though I dread doing so. I want to call Kris instead. I want to ask how Jason's doing. I want to hear about his first day of fifth grade, his lunch table, his new desk. I want to touch the top of his buzz cut and rub it for luck.

But I can't be in two places. Justin needs me more. Jason will understand. I hope.

Finally, I break down and call Mom.

"How is he?" she sobs.

She's unraveling. And I resent it. I've stayed strong for Justin. Isn't that what parents do? We hold it together. We don't fall apart when our kids are scared. Why can't she hold it together for me?

"He's getting transferred," I say, flatly.

"We're coming. I'm booking flights."

"Please don't. Just wait."

"I'm coming."

"Mom, please—"

"You never should've let him play football."

She hangs up. I stare at my phone. We hit a pothole. Justin moans.

• • •

At Children's Hospital, the air is stale, the walls tired, the linoleum dull. No bright colors. No cheer. I panic. This place is so different from the freshly painted pastel walls of where we just were. Did we make a horrible mistake by coming here?

Then a woman appears in the doorway, her voice gentle, melodic. She looks me in the eyes.

"How are you doing?"

She means it.

I fall into her arms and sob. She doesn't flinch. She holds me. Hands me tissues. Tells me what to expect. Doctors, social worker, a private room. I nod, grateful.

Harry finds us. I fall into him next. He pats my hip—three firm taps. A silent code: Stay strong.

• • •

The staff at Children's is different. Warm, focused. Competent. The nurses call Justin "buddy." They smile, move with calm purpose. One of them tapes bold signs in all caps to his bed and door:

NPO

NOTHING BY MOUTH INCLUDING MEDS

No food. No water. No medication. His pancreas needs total rest. It has been leaking toxic enzymes into his body. That's what's causing the pain. Now they know.

• • •

Fifteen hours later, scans are complete. The surgeons come in.

"The pancreas is cracked," they say. "We need to operate."

I blink. I thought you never touched the pancreas. I thought it was the angry organ. That's what they kept telling us yesterday.

What they don't say aloud, or in words I understand, is that without this surgery, he won't survive.

We're led to pre-op. We hold each other, crying in stiff green chairs. It's one of the few times I see Harry cry. Days of fear break like a dam.

After surgery, we collapse in the ICU waiting room.

A nurse gently encourages us to go home. "He won't remember this part," she says. "The meds will cover it."

Jason needs us. So do the dogs. And Mom and Dell are arriving soon.

We drive home in silence, fearful of leaving him but trusting the nurse's advice.

• • •

At home, I sit at the kitchen table, staring into my coffee. Mom and Dell will arrive today. I'm not sure what to expect. Based on her reaction by phone, she could be needy and emotional or angry and aggressive. With her, it's always unpredictable.

I think of a rare moment—Christmas, junior year of high school—when her unpredictability tilted in my favor. I'd bounced checks buying everyone gifts, including a fancy food processor for her. I confessed and held my breath, prepared for the explosion. But she didn't blow. She wrote a check, covered the fees, and never mentioned it again. It was a rare moment of grace and kindness.

But I can count those on one hand. Most of the time, she's not a comfort. She makes things harder. And right now, I don't have it in me to navigate that minefield.

I jump when my phone chirps.

"Mrs. Murphy? It's Jessica in ICU. Justin woke up and asked for you."

Exactly what I feared.

We rush back. When we arrive, he's asleep again, tubes and wires everywhere.

We sit by his bed. He drifts in and out, hallucinating. Spiders, snakes, tiny football players scoring touchdowns.

"Did you see that, Dad? He's gonna score!"

We cry. Then we laugh. It feels wrong. It also feels necessary. We're cracking open, releasing the pressure. Just a little.

Kris texts. Mom and Dell picked up Jason. They're all home. Jason would rather be with Kris, Scott, and Scotty. So would I.

I step into the hallway and call Mom.

• • •

The elevator doors slide open. Mom, Dell, and Jason stand clustered together at the center. Jason drops Mom's hand and runs to me, throwing his arms around my waist and pressing his face into my chest.

I kiss the top of his head, then glance up and meet Mom's eyes. They're wild and vacant all at once, darting around as if she's trying to make sense of her surroundings.

I hug them each in turn and lead them down the hallway to the ICU. Only immediate family are allowed inside, so Mom and Dell have to wait. My first priority is Jason. He hasn't seen Justin in days. It's the longest they've ever been apart.

Harry steps out of the ICU just as Jason and I step in, hand in hand, walking toward Justin's bed.

My heart breaks watching Jason's face register everything: the machines, the beeping, the sterile brightness, the tangled tubes. What I've become numb to, he's seeing for the first time. Through his eyes, I see it all anew. And it's horrifying.

Tears spill down his cheeks in heavy, silent drops. He swipes them away with the heels of his hands, trying so hard to be brave.

"Mrs. Murphy?"

I turn. A young woman stands behind me.

"Is this Justin's brother?" she asks gently.

"Yes, this is Jason."

She crouches to meet his eyes. "Hi, Jason. I'm Rebecca. I'm a social worker here at the hospital. I'm really glad you came today." Her voice is soft, calm, steady.

"I know it can be scary to see your brother like this—with all the tubes and machines. A lot of kids feel that way. It doesn't mean anything is wrong with you. It just means you love him and you're worried. You being here is really important. Even if Justin can't say it, hearing your voice or just knowing you're close can help him feel safe too."

Jason nods, still blinking back tears. Her words soothe both of us.

She leans in and whispers that it's best for Jason not to stay long. I nod, taking her guidance to heart.

Later that day, I run into Rebecca again. She tells me that typically siblings meet with a social worker *before* visiting the ICU. They're prepared, told what to expect, eased in.

My stomach sinks. I apologize, horrified that I tossed Jason into the fire without warning. I never would have done that if I'd known. No one told me. I hate that I didn't know. It's remarkable how I didn't even think to ask. I never do. I was conditioned to go forth and figure things out on my own.

•••

Harry and I begin rotating nightly shifts, so one of us can sleep at home and see Jason while the other stays with Justin. Mom and Dell settle in at our house, caring for Jason and the dogs.

One morning after my turn sleeping at home, I stumble downstairs, mindful that I need to hit the road soon, so I don't get stuck in traffic.

My yoga pants fall loosely on my frame. I feel them swish side to side around my hips as I walk. That never happens. Clothes always fit snug on my hips—tight—even when they're not supposed to. I've clearly lost weight. Stress does that. Plus, the cafeteria food looks awful, and I can't think of eating when there are so many other issues to worry about.

As I round the kitchen corner, I find Mom and Dell sitting quietly at our small maple table. I take in the scene: two plates of scrambled eggs, fresh fruit, and toasted English muffins buttered with strawberry jelly. Two glasses of orange juice. Two cups of coffee. Two napkins. Two sets of silverware. Breakfast for two. No third place setting.

I stop, staring at their spread.

"Morning."

"Morning," they both reply.

"Are you going to get something to eat?" Mom asks.

My heart sinks with disappointment. I would love nothing more than to sit down to a plate of eggs and fruit. Even if it means scarfing it down to beat the traffic. But there's no plate for me. No thought of me.

On the surface, it looks as if she's helping by being there for our family. But is she? I'm not even sure why she's here, other than to be able to tell others all she did to help. Her agenda always involves making herself look better.

I didn't even want her here. Jason was doing fine at Scott and Kris's house. Maybe doing better over there because he knows them so well. And the dogs were fine too, with daily visits, pee breaks, and feedings. Yet Mom was going to do what she wanted to do, without regard for me, my needs, or my wishes.

As I stare at their breakfasts, I see clearly that it's me who needs care now. And once again, she's not there for me. Not willing—never willing—to put my needs above hers. It feels personal. Like a rejection. Has she ever cared about me? Ever loved me? How hard would it have been to make one more plate?

Any decent person would have thought to feed someone experiencing this kind of stress. If it had been anyone else—anyone but me—she would've had a plate ready and waiting. She knows how to turn on the charm, how to be gracious and caring when it's in her own best interests. This is just one more glaring example of how she neglects me. And only me.

So yes, it is personal. And it's old, familiar, and ever so disappointing.

"I'll just grab a yogurt," I say, reaching into the fridge.

• • •

By Day Nine, Justin's been moved from the ICU to a private room. Over the next few days, we paper the walls with Get Well Soon messages—posters signed by his football and lacrosse teammates, banners from the wrestling team, cards and artwork from his elementary school classmates, and greetings from friends and family far away. Coaches visit. Friends bring groceries, salads, and snacks. And hugs. So many hugs. Our community is rallying around us, deeply loving us. And that means everything right now.

Through all of our years on fields and in gyms, at the local dive bar and tailgate parties, we've surrounded ourselves with like-minded people who care about what we care about. Family. And togetherness. We're not merely fitting in with this crowd. We belong.

Their outpouring of love and attention is contrasted by Mom's detachment and by her panicky, doe-eyed look. I recognize it as the same look I saw on Grandma's face the weekend we got married. While all of the family gathered in the living room for my bridal shower, Grandma stared at me like she didn't know who I was. Eyes darting back and forth, desperately trying to make sense of her surroundings. The faces. The noise. There, but not there.

I see that in Mom now. The inability to make sense of sights, sounds, smells, what's happening around her. The overwhelm caused by the chaos of beeping machines and scurried footsteps, and the stress of this moment.

Four days into her visit, it's all become too much for her. She's ready to go back to California, and I'm relieved.

I should feel more compassion in this moment, I tell myself. Especially if these are signs of dementia. But I don't. Plain and simple. I don't want to worry about or manage her on top of everything else. Justin is still far from ready to be discharged; doctors say it will be at least two more weeks.

That night, it's my turn to sleep at home. I thank them for coming and hug them goodbye. Their flight will leave in the morning, after I've already left for the hospital.

When Jason heads to bed, I follow him upstairs. After tucking him in, I linger, crawling in beside him. The moment the mattress cradles me, my body melts. My bones feel liquid, too heavy to hold me up. I lay my head on his chest, utterly spent.

He wraps an arm around me, and I can't help but weep. We lie there quietly until he speaks.

"Mom?" he says softly.

"Mm-hmm?"

"Justin's gonna be okay."

He sounds so certain, as if he knows something I don't. My heart clenches. Will Justin be okay? This ordeal has shown me just how much is beyond my control, beyond any parent's control.

Aren't I supposed to be the strong one—the one who consoles him, my sweet eleven-year-old? I shouldn't let him see me afraid, sad, overwhelmed. I should pull myself together. But I can't.

Maybe it's okay. Maybe letting him see me this way, letting him comfort me, is its own kind of strength. This is what I always wish Mom could do: be present and comforting.

Accepting Jason's kindness might be the best way to reinforce the kind of man I hope he becomes: someone who notices when others are struggling and steps in.

He could have met me tonight with resentment or jealousy; I wouldn't have blamed him. Instead, he's looking beyond himself, letting me lean on him.

I sink deeper into his chest and decide that it's okay for him to see me vulnerable.

"Yes, he is," I tell him. "He's going to be okay. We're all going to be okay."

Chapter 24

When I started my career, I would've been interested to learn how Mom handled misogynistic colleagues or unwanted advances—the hand on a kneecap under the table at a business lunch; the random, unwanted come-on by a colleague. She must've faced those situations. How did she navigate them as a young single woman in a male-dominated workplace?

Maybe she had personal-finance tips to share, especially about real estate investments. Or stories about growing up in El Paso. What was it like to defy her father's wishes and forge a big career rather than become a housewife? Did she ever feel like a groundbreaking feminist?

But I never asked those questions. And she never shared. Stories didn't tumble out. She wasn't self-reflective. Instead, I came to know her only by quiet observation. And what I noticed most was her penchant for volatility and destruction, even as she donned fine clothes and jewelry, tastefully decorated her homes, and nurtured gardens of eye-popping color. On the outside, she was veiled in beauty; on the inside brewed raging hostility.

Mom never knew me either. She still doesn't. Because she shows little interest, I'm not forthcoming. I close off myself, which is easy. She's too lost in her own thoughts, too preoccupied with work to notice anything about me or how I move through life.

Now that I'm a parent, all that I missed from our relationship—the stark void—is even more apparent, palpable. And though I fear tipping into the realm of parenting extremes when I overcompensate for what my own upbringing lacked, I double-down on what seems natural and intuitive. Namely, good parents show an interest. Good parents get to know their kids.

My friends and I pay attention to our children. We're wired to care for, know, protect, and nurture them. We're fascinated by who they are and who they're becoming. We want to know how they think, what they like, their moods, quirks, and dreams. Even the smallest milestone sparks curiosity, making me want to learn more, watch more, understand more.

I contemplate the effects of Mom's disinterest. And Dad's conspicuous absence. How their inability to be caring, curious, kind, loving, or present left me to fend for myself emotionally, and at times, physically. Their neglect surfaced a litany of questions: If my parents aren't interested in me, who will be? What does it mean if someone doesn't care enough to ask? Did I do something wrong to cause their absence and detachment?

With no clear answers or explanations, I learned to settle for surface-level exchanges that went against my nature. I became what I thought other people wanted me to be. A chameleon. But those early interactions and relationships were hollow and transactional, lacking the give-and-take rhythm of true connection. That is, until I began to read self-help books, scrutinize past relationships, assess my missteps, and work to break learned behaviors and generational patterns. In time and with practice, I discovered that meaningful relationships require curiosity, exchange, trust, and vulnerability.

I've worked hard to overcome my reticence and to develop connections, so much so that it now feels second-nature—with everyone except Mom.

When she visits, I prefer having Harry around. He prompts conversations I can't. Without him, she and I default to talking about books or the boys, until we sink into a quicksand of silence. The morass between us seems insurmountable.

• • •

Her diagnosis of mild cognitive impairment comes soon after Justin's injury and only confirms what we already suspect. By 2009, just four years later when she is only 69 years old, her memory and cognition are in steep decline. Yet, because so little tethers us together, it doesn't change much between us.

Dell and I begin to talk daily—sometimes multiple times. I'm his sounding board, the one he turns to as Mom's condition shifts. We discuss her behaviors, doctor appointments, caregiving aids, dental care, finances, wills and trusts, escalating symptoms, worries, fears, and frustrations. Each time we solve one issue, a new one arises. No solution is permanent. The frequent calls bring us closer. We're a real father-daughter team hand-in-hand navigating her health crisis.

After he'd confided to me a few years earlier that he was committed to his marriage to Mom, I stopped fearing he might leave her and that I might lose him. At some point, he then began introducing me as his daughter and I began introducing him as my dad. I also started referring to my biological father as Larry.

• • •

Every few months, I fly from Virginia to California to visit, to see how her illness is progressing. On this most recent trip, she and I sit at the small oak table in her kitchen.

She once obsessed over every detail of this space: limestone floors, marble counters, cherry cabinets. She'd made sure the architect designed a view that stretched from the sink through the atrium and living room all the way to the Pacific Ocean crashing against the bluff below.

"Kitchens are always designed by men," she huffed, "with no thought to how a cook moves." This kitchen was her statement on how design should be done—beautiful, functional, practical.

As we eat breakfast quietly, I taste salt air drifting in on the ocean breeze and hear the tinkling of wind chimes.

"How's Justin?" she asks. She remembers him best, her first grandchild.

"He's fine."

Minutes pass. I see her staring, as if forming a new thought.

"How's Justin?" she whispers again.

Sometimes, when she asks the same question repeatedly, I switch up my answers, hoping to divert the conversation down a new path. It rarely works. Today, I'm not much for games.

"He's good, Mom."

She stabs at her honeydew melon with a knife. It squirts across the plate. She tries again. And then once more. The woman who once helped launch satellites can no longer figure out how to use her utensils.

I pick up her fork and place it against her palm until she grasps it.

"Oh, okay," she murmurs. I watch her gaze down at her plate, taking note of how docile she is.

Gone is her belligerence, that cocksure certainty.

Her meanness and indifference left me no choice but to erect a wall between us. I wanted to know her better, but my fear of her also constrained me. The wall that once protected me is all but crumbling. I'm no longer afraid.

Still, I haven't found ways to connect with her. I'm not compelled to hold her hand or stroke her hair as one might see in the movies. I'm merely benefiting from her fading ability to inflict harm.

Her voice pierces the silence. "So, how's Justin?"

If her brain powered her cruelty, then her dementia is my cure.

How ironic that her brilliant mind is failing. Is it wrong of me to see her decline as a blessing? Had her body failed while her mind stayed sharp, she might still direct her anger at me and Dell. I imagine her in a wheelchair spewing venom from across the room.

Dementia provides a reprieve, yet still, I ponder: *What do we owe our parents in their hour of need if they neglected us as children?*

I also wonder how to separate feelings of obligation from a genuine desire to help. Does my motivation—or lack of it—matter? If I choose to help, how can I feel good about it rather than resentful or conflicted? Do I even want to care for her? Why would I?

On the other hand, if I decide not to help, can I live with that choice? Maybe there are ways to support her needs without compromising myself. I have no idea what that might look like.

On the flight home, questions linger. I'm pensive. Just because she can't wound me anymore doesn't mean I overflow with devotion. Love isn't something I can summon on command, no matter how much I might wish it. It's taken me a lifetime to figure out that love—the act of loving—is reciprocal.

Mom said she loved me, but she didn't show it. Her actions were in steep contrast to her words. I realize now that love is a tangible give-and-take, not a declaration tossed in someone's direction.

I decide to do only what feels right. I will be responsible and compassionate—even when the thought slips in that she hasn't earned the right for me to care. I'll push away those thoughts. They're petty, vengeful. That isn't who I am or who I want to be.

What matters most is continuing to be there for Dell. He is the father I always longed for, the only parent who's been there for me. Our relationship is what matters. Standing by him seems natural and true. That, more than anything, feels like love.

Chapter 25

Over the next ten years, Dell and I work together to manage Mom's care, with me serving as his confidant. As her needs change, we adjust our approach. First, we hire a local woman to be her companion so that Dell can run errands, go to the gym, and take occasional hikes in the nearby mountains. Tanya cooks meals, does laundry, and sits in the den chatting with Mom.

When Dell is scheduled for a hip replacement, I fly out for two weeks to help. I work on my laptop at the kitchen table, eyeing Tanya's interactions with Mom. Everyone outside the family makes it look so easy.

One day, Tanya washes and folds Mom's sheets.

"Have you seen how she folds sheets? Or makes the bed?" Mom asks with great earnestness.

"No, I haven't."

"I don't know how she does it." She sighs, wide-eyed.

Moments like this remind me how much she's declined. She was a brilliant scientist who also kept a spotless, near-perfect home. It never would have occurred to her to consider folding sheets or making beds as difficult or challenging. Now she marvels at tasks she once did without thinking. Worse, she's gushing over Tanya.

The heat of jealousy rises from my belly and lodges in my throat, burning my ears and cheeks. The hurt isn't about the sheets. It's the old ache:

her praise landing on someone else. As quickly as the emotions swell, I become angry for reacting. Why does it bother me that she's fawning over Tanya? This is how it's always been. When am I going to stop pining after the attention she offers others and has rarely extended to me? These wounds from childhood should have healed years ago; it's maddening each time they surface.

At night, after Mom is asleep, Dell and I sit in the den for hours talking about big topics—spirituality, family histories, work, and past relationships. Nothing is off limits.

I'd long ago shared what it was like growing up with Mom. He'd told me about his promise to himself, after two failed marriages, to make this one last. He was determined to stay by her side for the long haul, no matter what. He was committed and sincere.

• • •

When it's time for me to head home, Dell stands with me and Mom in the foyer.

"Isn't it great that Kim came all this way to help?"

"Mm-hmm." She nods.

"Don't you want to tell her?" he prompts.

She looks at me silently. After a few moments, knowing she isn't going to say anything, I break the tension, eager for the awkwardness to end.

"It's fine," I say, brushing off his pleas.

I'm grateful he knows that a thank-you and kind words are in order. He appreciates my efforts. I've left my family, put my life on hold, and re-arranged work schedules and projects.

How refreshing it would be to hear an acknowledgement from her. But it's not coming, and that recognition lands with a familiar sting. When will I accept the fact that this is who she is? This is how she treats me. How she's always treated me. The longer I'm a parent, the more it baffles me. Thankfully, in a few short hours, I'll be back home with Harry and the boys—far from her and back where I belong.

As Mom's needs evolve and her capabilities decline further, we cycle through everything from round-the-clock home care to memory-care facilities to private home-care settings. Dell devotes enormous time and energy to caring for her. She's so lucky to have him. I wouldn't have agonized the way he does. I'd likely have chosen a facility and visited occasionally. Or, more likely, we would've been estranged. Who knows how the story would have gone.

I'm lucky to have Dell too. Because he's devoted to her, I don't have to be. By supporting him, I'm indirectly supporting her. That lets me off the hook when I feel hard-edged or void of tenderness.

It's even a struggle for me to accept comfort from friends who tell me how sorry they are that my mother has dementia. Their eyes brim with empathy, as if I'm navigating something impossibly hard. My first instinct is to wave them off, to swat away their concerns.

"Oh, it's fine. Really, it's fine!" I want to say.

Instead, I stammer an awkward thank-you, guilty that I can't seem to summon the kind of grief or despair their kindness assumes I must feel.

• • •

Shortly after Dell called to say that Mom was likely to die soon, while Harry and I were driving to North Carolina, I decided I would fly out to be with them both. Within two days, I'm on a plane to California. After all these years navigating her illness together, I couldn't imagine not showing up for him. Or, knowing that if I didn't, he'd be all alone during her final moments. I couldn't let that happen.

I settle into my seat, open my laptop on the tray table, and begin typing. I'm not planning to speak at any funeral service we might hold, but I feel compelled to write some form of tribute. Isn't that what a good daughter would do? Perhaps more important, everyone deserves to have something written about them to summarize their time and impact on this earth after they die.

While our relationship was complicated, I can't deny that she lived on her own terms, made significant contributions to the betterment and security of our country, and forged a path for women in engineering and science. She was a woman of many interests and considerable skill.

I want to be the kind of daughter who can casually fill a legal pad with fond memories. I want to be shattered with grief, undone by loss—like

Cheryl Strayed in *Wild*, spiraling after her mother's death and driven to walk for months on the Pacific Crest Trail just to survive the pain. Unfortunately, that's not me.

From my blue faux-leather seat on a Southwest flight, somewhere above the Midwest, I stare out at the clouds. Whatever I write has to be honest, not a collection of soft-focus platitudes. But how do you write a tribute to someone—your mother, no less—when you're not sorry she's dying?

•••

The seatbelt light blinks on and the captain's voice fills the cabin; we'll be landing soon. Over the five-hour flight, I've managed to wrangle a draft I can live with. I close my laptop and stow my backpack beneath the seat in front of me. After we land, I take a taxi to the facility where she's been for the past many months. It's not a true facility, but rather a regular three-bedroom, two-bath suburban home tucked in a cul-de-sac in Redwood City, blocks from the heart of Silicon Valley.

Nothing from outside the house signals that terminal patients are being cared for around the clock by a cadre of Filipino women and men, who take turns changing diapers, dispensing medications, washing sheets, and cooking meals. The living room is lined with sleeping bags flopped atop mattresses on the floor, where caregivers sleep. She's fortunate to have the primary bedroom all to herself.

I tiptoe through the foyer and down the hall to Mom's room. Dell and Uncle Bob, Mom's youngest brother, are there. I give each of them hugs. We sit quietly, catching up for a few minutes, then look alternately at Mom in the bed or down at our phones. She's been like this for a few years: bedridden, eyes closed, not speaking. She appears waif-like beneath the bedspread, yet her latte-colored skin is smooth and creamy.

She would despise this. How she's been incapacitated for so long, unable to live a dynamic or interesting life. How she's been at the mercy of others to wash her hair, brush her teeth, and wipe her ass. How she's simply existed, day after day, in pajamas or sweatpants. No makeup or lipstick, no jangling jewels or baubles, no spicy-scented perfumes or silk blouses.

I think back to a dinner years ago, when Harry and I visited California early in our marriage. Mom was already nursing fears of getting dementia or Alzheimer's after watching Grandma suffer.

"If that happens to me, I want Dell to roll me to the blufftop in my wheelchair and push me over!" She was serious. It was a command.

I laughed. "Oh my god, Mom, don't be ridiculous. He can't do that. It would be illegal."

As we argued, she became more agitated and strident. Finally, we dropped the conversation and cleared our plates.

So yes, she would have hated all of this. In some ways, we took such great care of her, allowing her to stay at home with around-the-clock care for so many years that perhaps we prolonged the inevitable. We'd created an environment where no germs could afflict her, without which she'd certainly have died sooner. In staving off bladder infections, pneumonia, and bedsores, our interventions caused her to live longer, forcing a long, slow death.

• • •

Later that night, Dell retreats to a local hotel room to get some sleep. He's exhausted by the years of caregiving, but especially by the intensity of the past few days. Preparing yourself for death to come, day after day, takes a toll.

I sit at her bedside and gently take her hand in mine. I stroke the raised blue vein running down the back of her hand from her wrist to her middle finger. Rubbing it softly, rhythmically, I recall all the moments as a little girl I held these hands. I could be anywhere and close my eyes and be able to see her hands vividly. Absent from her left hand is her large diamond wedding ring and the small pinky ring from her favorite aunt that I used to twirl around her finger when I sat on her lap as a child. Both are now tucked away safely in a jewelry box at home.

As I slump in my chair, I think back over moments from our past. Twenty-five years earlier, I'd struggled over what to buy her for Christmas one year. I couldn't afford any jewelry, artwork, clothing, or pottery that she might like. She was impossible to shop for. I'd pondered the dilemma as I dumped the boys' clean laundry from the basket onto the couch. One by one, I folded pairs of Scooby-Doo underwear, footie pajamas, and brightly colored pocket T-shirts in size small, tossing them into separate piles on the cushion.

From behind me, I heard Oprah talking up the holiday's best gift ideas. As she and her guests chatted, one idea caught my attention. It was a thoughtful and inexpensive keepsake gift. And it could be homemade! The idea? A gift box containing handwritten notes extolling the virtues and memories you love most about the recipient.

It seemed easy enough but proved much harder to fill the box than expected. *What do I love about her?* I kept asking myself. Few answers sprang to mind. I sat tapping my chin, staring off toward the bookshelves, hoping one of the limp ivy plants three tiers up might whisper a clue.

Her hands. Yes, her hands. I loved them. Delicate yet strong and capable. They pulled weeds in the garden, installed dimmer switches throughout the house, spritzed perfume lightly on her collarbones, hung strips of beef jerky from drying racks, and sewed my grade-school rompers.

They were busy hands, even when she was at rest, which was typically only if she was confined to the passenger seat of a car—like when my second father, Tom, would drive the three of us to flower farms forty minutes away in Half Moon Bay so that she could buy plants; or later, when her boyfriend Jim drove us to his weekend cabin in Fall River.

From the backseat, I'd hear the *swish-swish-swish* of her emery board filing each nail to a sharp point, defying the prevailing beauty standard of softer, rounded shapes. I loved it when she used those spiky nails to softly tickle my cheeks with a gentle clawing motion.

"I have always loved your hands," I scribbled on the note card and dropped it into the box. One note down. Nine more to go. Eventually, I completed all ten note cards, though none of the sentiments were as sincere as that first one.

I look down at our clasped hands. Her eyes are closed, her breathing shallow and intermittent. I lay my head on her leg and weep quietly into the blankets. After all these years, my pent-up resentments and dogged dreams are pouring forth.

Her passing will mark the end of hope: no more opportunities for us to transform into a mother-daughter duo; no more slim chances that our relationship might be something other than what it is. Our story ends here.

And yet, were it not for my resentments and judgments about her, maybe I wouldn't have been so motivated to be different than she was. Maybe I wouldn't have taught myself how to build a lasting, loving marriage. Or fought so hard to find a way to balance work and parenting. Or understood the power of simply being there for those I love.

I can trace everything I have, everything I am to how I was mothered. I didn't want to be anything like her and worked hard to correct what I viewed as her wrongs and failings, especially when it came to marriage and family. In doing so, I *unmothered* myself, rejecting the self-centeredness she modeled and undoing the damage of years of neglect and abuse at her hands. Only then was I able to become the woman and parent I intended to be––independent of yet also driven by the pains, loneliness, and losses of my childhood.

Do I have my own long list of failures? Of course. Yet, I am confident that despite my many mistakes, Harry and the boys know how much I love them, and I know how much they love me. The same could not be said for Mom and me.

• • •

The day after she dies, I'm perched in bed with swollen eyes and a throbbing headache. With my laptop resting on my thighs, I check my email and let people know I'll be out of the office for a few days.

I decide to send Larry an email to tell him Mom has passed. While I haven't seen him since my Florida trip more than thirty years ago, we've exchanged Christmas cards, as well as occasional letters and emails. Once or twice a year, I send photos of the boys with newsy updates.

In my note to him, I share the tribute I wrote on the plane. Before sending it, I delete the line that says she left him because she wanted more than a husband with little ambition who drank too much.

There's no need to hurt anyone's feelings.

He replies quickly. And his feelings are hurt, over a different line I failed to scrub. The one stating she married as a way to escape her patriarchal home.

His response to me is blistering.

He tells me I know only one side of the story. That there's a lot I don't know about Mom. Like, for instance, that she slept with her boss to get a promotion. That he chose to take the high road when he found out. Perhaps he should have shot that guy like he'd planned. He tells me he's still bitter more than fifty-five years and two marriages later.

I slide beneath the covers and read his response again and again. Each time, my heart races faster. The throbbing in my head gets louder, echoing in my ears. The entire email is about him. His grievances. His feelings. His years of anger.

My head swells with thoughts. I'm not surprised in the least by the details he divulges. I knew she had affairs with married men. Phil couldn't have been the only one. I knew she was shrewd and calculating.

What I'm surprised by is his deep narcissism. I am his daughter. And I'm only twenty-four hours from losing my mother. Other than what I wrote in my tribute, he has no idea what type of relationship we had or how devastated I might be to learn his version of events. Clearly, he doesn't care one bit about me or my feelings, or how his disclosure might affect me.

My whole life, I believed Mom when she told me that I was just like him. Although I never quite knew what she meant, I wore her insult as a badge of honor because I didn't want to be anything like her. Now I see that he and I are nothing alike.

But he and Mom were. They were both selfish and self-absorbed.

I rattle off a quick response to him, letting him know he's not the only one Mom hurt or betrayed. I tell him to get in line. I explain I've spent a lifetime thinking we were similar but have finally discovered that's not at all true. We're nothing alike. I end the email with one clear statement: *When I bury Mom, I will also bury my relationship with you.*

I press Send, vowing never to waste another minute on him.

All day, his words and mine tumble in my head, along with a lifetime of memories. Building Christmas villages in the stone fireplace with Mom. Catching colors with Carolyn in the car. Smelling alcohol's tangy-sweet scent on Larry's breath. Being dragged across the family room floor and kicking Mom in the stomach. Enjoying lunch with Justin and Dell.

Through the kaleidoscope of moments, I see how deeply flawed my biological parents were, and how my stepparents, Carolyn and Dell, gave me the love I craved and deserved. Yet even though they showed how loving parents should act, I continued to look to Mom and Larry to do the same, chasing their attention at every turn and forever hoping they would change. That deep human yearning to be cared for, loved by, and seen by your parents blinded me to a stark reality: They were incapable of providing what I wanted or needed.

I was never going to find it where I was searching.

The final scene of *The Wizard of Oz*, my favorite childhood movie, rushes to mind. I watch Dorothy in her bed, surrounded by Aunt Em, Uncle Henry, and the others—significant people in her life who weren't actually her parents. She realizes that what she's yearned for was with her all along. There's no place as dear or as comforting as her own home, she says.

I pick up my cellphone and place a call.

"Hi, hon," Harry says.

Acknowledgements

To my dear friend and writing partner Laura—Thank you for dedicating hundreds of hours to read and review my work. This book would not exist without our infinite "Sorry, not sorry" conversations where you urged me to go deeper. I am forever grateful to you—and for you—and so incredibly proud of what we've achieved on our respective writing journeys. No doubt, we are better together!

www.ingramcontent.com/pod-product-compliance
Lightning Source LLC
Chambersburg PA
CBHW020957160726
47994CB00006B/2265